7 SECRET PILLARS OF SOBRIETY

WHAT TO DO WHEN AA AND 12 STEPS AREN'T FOR YOU

BY

TIM MURPHY

For more information or to contact us directly:

mailto:7pillarsofsobriety@gmail.com

mailto:https://www.7secretpillarsofsobriety.com/

ISBN - Paperback: 978-1-998585-31-1

ISBN – Hardcover: 978-1-965146-21-7

DISCLAIMER

The content provided in this book is designed to provide helpful information on the subjects discussed. This book is not meant to be used, nor should it be used, to diagnose or treat any medical condition. The claims in this book are theoretical and to be used for illustrative purposes only. The publisher and the authors are not responsible for any actions you take or do not take as a result of reading this book, and are not liable for any damages or negative consequences from action or inaction to any person reading or following the information in this book. References are provided for informational purposes only and do not constitute endorsement of any websites or other sources. Readers should also be aware that the websites listed in this book may change or become obsolete.

FOREWORD

In today's landscape, where the journey to sobriety is increasingly acknowledged as a deeply personal and multifaceted endeavor, it is vital to explore and embrace methods that extend beyond conventional frameworks. *7 Secret Pillars to Sobriety* stands out as a crucial resource in this regard. This book is not just a guide but a beacon of hope, offering practical and innovative approaches for those navigating the path to sobriety with personalized, alternative methods.

Traditional AA and 12-step programs, while beneficial for many, do not always resonate with everyone, even those with a sincere desire to live alcohol-free. Tim Murphy's experience epitomizes this challenge. Faced with the limitations of conventional methods, Tim embarked on a quest for a different approach to recovery. His journey led him to explore, adapt, and refine his strategies, culminating in the invaluable insights shared within these pages.

7 Secret Pillars to Sobriety is a comprehensive treasure trove of Tim's personal strategies and methods, offering innovative solutions for those who, like him, have struggled to find success in traditional programs. Each chapter meticulously addresses crucial aspects of the sobriety process, from committing fully to your sobriety goals and utilizing visualization techniques to building a supportive network. The inclusion of practical tools such as daily journaling, gratitude practices, and positive affirmations highlights a holistic approach designed to motivate and guide you toward success. In my nearly 15 years of Emotional Sobriety research and training development, I see this as a necessary starting point to take full ownership of your sobriety and therefore, life.

Tim Murphy's candid and vulnerable sharing of his own journey provides a powerful and relatable context for the principles outlined in this book. His personal narrative offers inspiration and validation, reminding you that sobriety is a highly individual journey, yet you're not alone in your struggles.

What distinguishes this book is its focus on resilience and adaptability critical elements for overcoming the challenges of sobriety. The actionable takeaways and clear calls to action offer a structured roadmap for you to integrate these principles into your daily life, fostering sustainable sobriety. There is no lasting sobriety without sustainability.

In reading *7 Secret Pillars to Sobriety,* you will not only gain effective strategies and techniques but also a profound sense of empowerment and hope. Tim Murphy's process and commitment makes this book an invaluable resource for those seeking to carve out their own path from insobriety to freedom.

May this book inspire, guide, and support you on your journey to lasting health and personal growth. Tim's dedication to your success is evident, and his belief in your potential is clear. Embrace the wisdom within these pages and take proactive steps towards your recovery, knowing that you are worth every effort.

I can almost hear him say in the voice of support and confidence in you get to work.

Dr. Andrea Vitz, D.C

Emotional Sobriety Expert

Co-founder, Lifted Academy

Endorsements

"7 Secret Pillars of Sobriety" provides a transformative approach to sobriety, extending its principles to various aspects of life. It offers deep insights and strategies for personal growth, making it valuable for those seeking sobriety and those aiming to live a more intentional and fulfilling life.

Jason Howe, Best-selling author UNLEASHED and Executive Director, K9s On the Front Line

"7 Secret Pillars of Sobriety is a transformative guide for anyone seeking a new approach to sobriety beyond traditional methods. As someone who values personal growth, I found the principles in this book incredibly applicable to various aspects of life. Each pillar offers profound insights and universally empowering strategies. This book is not just for those seeking sobriety; it's for anyone committed to living a more intentional and fulfilled life. A must-read for discovering new paths to personal empowerment.

Kristin Gutierrez, Bestselling Author and Founder of Million DollarOfferChallenge.com

If you are struggling to find sobriety and the "traditional" methods have not worked for you, this book is the key to accomplishing your goal. Perfectly created, Tim's methods are an alternative to finding a purposeful life through sobriety.

Forgiving Unforgivable, LLC, Author, Attorney, Mediator

7 Secret Pillars of Sobriety is a powerful testament to the human spirit's resilience in the face of addiction. As a life transformation coach, I am deeply impressed by the author's raw honesty and introspection. This book offers a transformative roadmap and a fresh perspective on recovery, challenging traditional methods and their innovative approach to recovery. This book stands out by offering a comprehensive toolkit for sustainable sobriety, including goal setting, accountability partnerships, and daily practices like

journaling and gratitude exercises. The author's emphasis on personalized strategies and environmental adjustments resonates deeply with effective life coaching principles. What truly sets this work apart is its actionable takeaways-from visualizing success to developing trigger management plans. This is a well-laid-out roadmap to lasting change. For anyone seeking to transform their relationship with addiction, this book provides the insights, strategies, and encouragement needed to embark on a fulfilling life of passion and purpose!

Annette Weiss

Expert Life Transformation Coach

Published Author

PublishSpeakandProsper.com

Wow, "What to Do When AA and 12 Steps Aren't for You" the subtitle blew me away. I truly thought everyone would resonate with the famous "12-step" program. But now... now I'm enlightened. One can tell that Tim has been there and done that, and in each of the 10 chapters, his practical knowledge, expertise, experience, and passion come out. In chapter 4, Tim talks about "making gratitude a daily habit," which is truly so important and alone can be life-changing, but he doesn't stop there. He gives a step-by-step way of implementing each of the pillars, which is very important.

7 Secret Pillars of Sobriety will change lives, there's no doubt about it. This is a book to read and read again and again!

Sensei Dave Armstrong, author of Why Me My Fight for Life, Owner and CEO at Inspire To Aspire Youth Empowerment and Unlimited Potential Network Academy, Coaching

In his book Seven Secrets Pillars of Sobriety, Tim Murphy provides a refreshing perspective for seeking alternatives to traditional AA and 12-step programs. By simplifying the often overwhelming 12-step approach into seven clear and actionable secrets, Tim addresses the age-old problem of addiction recovery with innovative and practical solutions.

Paul T. Neustrom, Author, Speaker, and Marketing and Sales Coach

NeuStream Media/ Founder - #1 International Best-Selling Author

TABLE OF CONTENTS

INTRODUCTION:
THE SOBRIETY REVOLUTION

The Growing Need for Alternative, Personalized Sobriety Methods Beyond Traditional Programs

There's a noticeable shift in how we approach the concept of recovery from addiction. For many years, traditional programs such as Alcoholics Anonymous and other 12-step models have dominated the landscape of sobriety support. These programs have undoubtedly been lifesavers for numerous individuals. However, they may not resonate with everyone. The reasons vary widely. Some people may not connect with the spiritual underpinnings of these programs, while others might find the group settings intimidating or unhelpful for their personal situations.

The world is diverse, and so are the people in it. This diversity means that the paths to recovery can be just as varied. Recognizing this, there's a growing understanding that we need more tailored approaches to sobriety. These methods consider the individual's unique background, circumstances, and needs. It's not just about providing more options; it's about providing the right options for the right people at the right time.

Why is this shift important? Imagine a scenario where everyone wore the same size shoes. Clearly, this wouldn't work comfortably for most. Similarly, when we acknowledge that one-size-fits-all solutions are not feasible for something as complex as human recovery, we begin to see the value in offering a variety of recovery tools and methods. This is where the concept of a sobriety revolution begins not just altering the existing methods but revolutionizing the way we think about and approach sobriety altogether.

Empowerment is a powerful tool. When individuals feel empowered, they take more active roles in their sobriety journey. This proactive involvement can make a significant difference in maintaining long-term sobriety. Empowerment in this context means providing the resources and support necessary for individuals to make informed choices about their recovery paths. How do we empower these individuals? First, by recognizing and validating their feelings and experiences. This validation helps remove the stigma and shame often associated with addiction, making it easier for individuals to step forward and seek help. Next, it involves offering choices. When people are given a range of recovery options, they are more likely to find a method that resonates with them personally, which increases their commitment to the process. It's also about providing continuous support. Recovery is not a one-time event but a lifelong journey. Continuous support might look like follow-up programs, community-building activities, or digital platforms for sharing experiences and successes. This ongoing engagement helps individuals feel connected and supported, reducing the sense of isolation that can sometimes accompany recovery.

This new empowerment perspective is not about discarding traditional methods but rather about expanding our toolkit. It's about creating a robust framework that supports every individual's journey toward sobriety. This inclusive, flexible, and non-judgmental approach is at the heart of the sobriety revolution. It acknowledges that while the goal is the same long-term sobriety the paths can be as diverse as the individuals walking them.

Ultimately, this revolution in sobriety care is about more than just combating addiction; it's about building a supportive community that values every individual's journey. It respects and celebrates the uniqueness of each journey, providing a tapestry of options that can be tailored to suit individual needs and circumstances. This is the essence of the sobriety revolution a movement that not only aims to change how we achieve sobriety but also how we perceive and support those who are on their way to recovery.

The sobriety revolution is about change. It's about challenging the status quo and advocating for a more personalized, empowering approach to recovery. By doing so, we not only increase the likelihood of successful long-term sobriety but also foster a broader societal acceptance of different recovery paths. This change is essential, as it acknowledges the complexity of addiction and the need for a more nuanced, compassionate approach to overcoming it.

As you begin this book, remember that each page is a step forward in understanding and embracing this new approach to sobriety. Together, we can be part of a significant change, contributing to a world where recovery is viewed through a lens of empathy, understanding, and personal empowerment. Welcome to the sobriety revolution.

My Journey to Sobriety

I grew up in a household where addiction cast a long shadow over everyday life. My parents struggled with alcohol, which deeply affected the atmosphere of our home. It wasn't easy. Each day brought new challenges as I tried to navigate through the mood swings and unpredictable behavior that often accompany heavy drinking. The environment was volatile, with tensions running high and resolution seeming distant. The impact of living in such a setting shaped my perceptions, my reactions to stress, and my understanding of normalcy. I learned to tread carefully, to gauge moods, and to anticipate outbursts. These were my early survival skills in my day-to-day world. They instilled in me a deep-seated resolve not to follow the same path as my parents. Despite this young promise, to myself the cycle of addiction is a tough one to break, and without realizing it, I began walking down that familiar road.

As I grew older, not only my home environment, but my social settings and peer influences exposed me to alcohol. It began innocently enough, as is often the case. A drink here, a party there; it seemed like a natural part of growing up. Unlike my home environment, it was fun to have a drink with friends. But as time went on, what was once occasional became frequent, and frequent turned into daily. I found myself relying on alcohol to unwind, to feel confident, or simply to feel normal. This gradual increase wasn't shocking; given my background. It was almost expected. Yet, each step took me further from who I wanted to be. The turning point came one night that remains a blur in memory but crystal clear in its consequences. I had been bar hopping, a regular activity by then, and on my way home, I blacked out and drove the car into the median. I hit the divided highway sign so perfectly that

4

it fell precisely down the middle of the car. It looked like I had done it on purpose. The sign crushed the top of the car down on me nearly cutting it and metaphorically, my life in two. It was a miracle I survived, let alone managed to drive myself the rest of the way home. Staring at the mangled car, that night, I finally acknowledged that I had to change. I realized I was self-destructing just like my parents.

My decision to seek help led me to Alcoholics Anonymous (AA), the most readily available resource. AA's approach with its meetings and step-based system was a beacon for many like me. I committed to the recommended 90 meetings in 90 days. In theory, this should have set me on a path to recovery. Yet, something didn't sit right. Despite my dedication, I felt a disconnect. The method, while supportive in offering a community, seemed too rigid, too prescriptive. It was as if the personal aspects of my struggle were being forced into a pre-shaped mold that didn't quite fit. The traditional methods of AA, while beneficial for some, emphasized a collective identity of addiction that overshadowed personal stories and individual recovery needs. Those methods didn't resonate with me. I needed something that acknowledged my personal journey, that recognized the unique elements of my struggle with addiction, and that equipped me with tools tailored to my specific circumstances. I needed to feel seen and heard.

The realization that a one-size-fits-all solution wasn't effective for everyone became a cornerstone in my recovery and later, my mission to help others. It was clear that I needed a different approach a more personalized path to sobriety that took into account my varied and complex life. This need led me to explore other options, to educate myself on addiction, and to understand its deep-seated causes and varying manifestations. I dove into research, spoke with experts, and most importantly, listened to many others who, like me, found traditional methods lacking.

My journey to sobriety was not linear. It involved many trials and errors, introspection, and a relentless pursuit of a program that acknowledged the personal aspect of recovery. Each step forward was hard-earned and each setback, a lesson. Over time, these experiences coalesced into a broader understanding of what effective recovery could involve. This understanding eventually culminated in the development of a transformative approach to sobriety one that I designed not only for my own recovery but to assist others in their battles against addiction. If I needed that, might other people as well?

This comprehensive, flexible, and non-judgmental sobriety program is what I now advocate. It is a testament to the belief that while addiction may be a common struggle, the road to recovery is distinctly personal. My journey underscores the importance of adapting recovery efforts to individual needs, ensuring that each person can find a path to sobriety that truly resonates with them and sustains their recovery in the long term.

In sharing my story, my hope is to reach others who may find themselves where I once was feeling misaligned with traditional recovery methods and seeking a solution that speaks directly to them. It's a reminder that although the journey is challenging and deeply personal, you are not alone, and more importantly, recovery is possible with the right approach tailored to your unique story. The lessons I've learned along the way are not just about overcoming addiction but also about understanding oneself and growing from the struggles faced. This book aims to provide not only insights into an alternative approach to sobriety but also practical tools that readers can adapt to their own lives, ensuring that the journey to recovery is a successful and lasting one.

A Transformative Approach

When we talk about overcoming challenges like addiction, the usual paths people think about are those that have existed for decades. As mentioned previously, programs like AA and other 12-step methods have been the go-to solutions. They have certainly helped many. But, there is more than one way to find the path to recovery.

First, let's redefine what we should really mean by cure: A cure is often considered a substance or procedure that ends a medical condition, like medication, surgery, a lifestyle change, or even a shift in mindset that alleviates suffering; it represents the state of being healed or cured. This medical condition could be anything from a disease, mental illness, or genetic disorder to something socially undesirable, like baldness. An incurable disease isn't necessarily terminal; likewise, a curable illness can still result in death.

But let's challenge this traditional view. Being cured is as much about your mindset as it is about medical intervention. If you can go about your life, attend social events, and meet friends at bars without any issues, you can consider yourself cured. If you can't, then it's clear you have more work to do. This isn't about what a dictionary says; it's about how you choose to live your life after sobriety.

This is where the idea of a more transformative approach comes into play. What I propose here is something more flexible, more personal and permanent solution. It does not judge; it supports. It does not dictate; it guides. This approach allows people to integrate recovery into their daily lives in a way that feels natural and sustainable for them. Why is this important? Because when recovery feels less like a prescribed set of actions and more like a personal journey, the likelihood of long-term success increases.

One of the core aspects of this transformative approach is focusing on personal growth and self-reflection. These are not just buzzwords; they are powerful tools. Personal growth involves improving one's self-awareness, developing talents, and potential. Self-reflection is about taking time to think deeply about your behaviors, beliefs, and values. By combining these, individuals can gain insights into what triggers their addictive behaviors and how to manage or avoid these triggers. More importantly, this process helps individuals rebuild their self-esteem and identity, which are often damaged by addiction.

Integrating recovery into everyday life is crucial. This means finding ways to make sobriety a natural part of your routine and your decision-making processes. It involves setting up a daily structure that supports sobriety but also feels fulfilling and engaging. This could mean adopting new hobbies, strengthening relationships with supportive friends or family, or even changing your environment to reduce temptations.

Flexibility is a significant factor. Traditional recovery programs often have a set schedule and strict rules that might not work for everyone. In a transformative approach, the idea is to create a plan that can adapt to changes in your life and your emotional state. This also means being open to trying different methods and strategies until you find what works best for you. Furthermore, the non-judgmental aspect of this approach is vital. Addiction can bring with it a lot of shame and guilt. A recovery program that avoids judgment and focuses on encouragement and understanding can help alleviate these feelings. It's about creating a supportive environment where failures are seen as part of the journey, not the end of it.

To implement such a program, one might start by defining clear, achievable goals. These goals should be specific and tailored to your personal needs. They should also be flexible enough to change as you grow and learn more about yourself. Regular self-reflection is important too. This could be through journaling, meditation, or therapy sessions. These practices help maintain a focus on personal growth and address any new challenges that arise.

Lastly, it's crucial to build a support system of people that love and want the best for you. This could include friends, family, therapists, or people who are on a similar journey. This network will provide encouragement, offer advice, and help keep you accountable. Remember, the goal of the transformative approach is not just to quit a substance but to build a life where you no longer feel you need that substance.

Therefore, a transformative approach to sobriety is about more than just stopping substance use; it's about changing your life. It's about understanding and nurturing yourself so deeply that sobriety becomes a part of who you are, not just something you do. This approach respects that everyone's journey is different and provides the tools to create a personalized path to recovery. It offers a promising alternative for those who find traditional methods challenging and seeks a deeply personal and empowering route to recovery. The 7 SECRET PILLARS OF SOBRIETY aligns with this personalized approach for those who feel that AA and 12-step programs are not for them.

Chapters Overview

Let's walk through what you can expect from each chapter of this book. Each one is crafted to help you on your path to sobriety with specific, easy-to-follow steps.

Chapter 1: Pillar # 1 Embracing 100% Commitment

Commitment is key in any journey, especially in the journey toward sobriety. This chapter talks about what it means to be fully committed. It's not just a promise to yourself; it's about setting a foundation for your entire recovery process. You will learn how to focus your energy and intentions, making sure every action supports your sobriety goals.

Chapter 2: Pillar # 2 Announcing Your Sobriety Goal

Sharing your goal can boost your motivation and help you find support. This chapter guides you through the process of sharing your sobriety goal with others in a way that feels safe and supportive. It discusses choosing the right people to tell and how their support can help you stay on track.

Chapter 3: Pillar # 3 Engaging in Daily Journaling

Keeping a journal helps you understand your thoughts and feelings better. In this chapter, you will discover the benefits of daily journaling. It shows how writing down your thoughts each day can serve as a stress reliever and a tool for self-reflection. You will get tips on how to start your journaling habit and how to make it a regular part of your day.

Chapter 4: Pillar # 4 Practicing Gratitude

Gratitude can transform your mindset positively. This chapter explores the practice of gratitude and its benefits. It offers practical tips on how to cultivate gratitude daily and how acknowledging the good in your life can change the way you see yourself and your recovery.

Chapter 5: Pillar # 5 Embracing Forgiveness

Forgiveness is a powerful tool for healing. Here, you will learn about the importance of forgiving yourself and others. The chapter provides steps to release anger and resentment, which are crucial for your emotional and mental health. It also discusses how forgiveness can lead to personal growth and a more fulfilling life.

Chapter 6: Pillar # 6 Harness the Power of Visualization

Visualization is the practice of picturing something in your mind. Creating a vision that motivates and inspires you to make those changes a reality. It's a transformational practice that can lead you to a more fulfilled and successful life.

Chapter 7: Pillar # 7 Utilize Positive Affirmations

Crafting personalized, concise statements directly tied to your sobriety goals can be immensely impactful. Affirmations, when consistently repeated, have the potential to reshape your thinking and transform your life. Tailor them thoughtfully to reflect your deepest aspirations, particularly in your journey toward sobriety.

Each chapter is designed to be a step that builds upon the previous one, creating a comprehensive path towards lasting sobriety. By the end of this book, you will have a deep understanding of the tools and practices needed to maintain your sobriety and grow personally. Each chapter not only explains the significance of these practices but also guides you on how to integrate them into your daily life effectively.

Now, let's embark on this journey together, with each chapter offering you practical strategies and heartfelt support. The chapters are more than just lessons; they are stepping stones to a new, empowered you. By the time you turn the final page, you will have everything you need to maintain your sobriety and live a life filled with health, happiness, and fulfillment.

This book is designed to act as a companion in your journey, a guide that you can return to whenever you need support or inspiration. Remember, the path to recovery is a marathon, not a sprint, and every small step you take is a part of a larger journey towards a happier, healthier you.

Let's move forward together with clarity and purpose, embracing each new day as an opportunity to strengthen your commitment to sobriety and personal growth.

CHAPTER ONE: PILLAR # 1 EMBRACE 100% COMMITMENT

Defining Your Sobriety Goal

When we talk about establishing a goal for sobriety, the first step is to set clear and measurable milestones. These milestones act as markers on your journey to sobriety, helping you visualize progress and stay motivated. For example, if your ultimate goal is to remain sober for a year, you might set a milestone for each month that passes without alcohol. Each of these monthly achievements serves not only as a testament to your commitment but also as a firm foundation for the next month.

It is crucial that these milestones are not just vague ideas but are specifically defined with timelines. Why is this important? Because when you set a date or a specific time frame for your milestones, it creates a sense of urgency and accountability. You know exactly what you need to achieve and by when, which makes it easier to stay on track. For instance, instead of saying, "I want to stop-drinking," you could set a milestone such as, "I will take my last alcoholic drink on a set date." This clarity helps in monitoring your progress and adjusting actions if necessary.

The next part of defining your sobriety goal involves creating a vivid, emotionally compelling vision of your sober life. What does this mean? It means visualizing how your life will improve once you achieve sobriety. Imagine waking up feeling energized and clear-headed every morning, or think about the relationships you could mend or strengthen when alcohol no longer controls your interactions. This vision should be detailed and filled with positive images of your future a future where you are not defined by your addiction but are free to live your best life.

Creating this vivid vision is not just an exercise in daydreaming. It serves a very practical purpose. Whenever you face temptations or setbacks as you inevitably will on this journey the vision of a sober life acts as a powerful motivator. It is a reminder of why you started this path in the first place and what you stand to gain by sticking to your commitment. Every choice to abstain, every milestone reached, brings you one step closer to making this vision a reality.

Moreover, emotionally compelling visions are linked to stronger resilience. Remember the old adage, "You are what you think about". When you can emotionally connect with the benefits of a sober life, you are more likely to push through difficult moments. This connection fosters a mindset that views sobriety not as a loss of something enjoyable (alcohol) but as the gain of something much more valuable health, happiness, and fulfillment.

You also need to develop social supports for yourself. A support group for alcoholism is at best a collective of individuals, selected by the person dealing with alcohol dependency, who come together to offer mutual encouragement, understanding, and support. These groups create a safe and empathetic environment where members can share their experiences, challenges, and successes in overcoming alcohol dependency. The primary goals are to foster a sense of community, reduce feelings of isolation, and promote personal growth and recovery through mutual aid. You then benefit from the genuine care and support of others who are committed to your well-being and dedicated to helping you maintain sobriety.

Let's summarize what we've covered: establishing clear, measurable sobriety milestones with specific timelines helps create structure and accountability. Additionally, crafting a vivid, emotionally compelling vision of your sober life enriches your motivation and resilience. These steps are not just about stopping something harmful but are about starting a new, enriched phase of life. They are about transformation and growth, about reclaiming control and rediscovering joy. By defining your sobriety goal with both precision and passion, you lay down a solid foundation for your journey to a happier, healthier you.

Setting sobriety goals is not just about avoiding alcohol but about creating a clear path towards the life you wish to lead. It is a proactive and positive approach to personal recovery and growth. Each milestone achieved is a victory not just over alcohol but over the constraints it placed on your life and relationships. And every day spent sober is a step closer to realizing the vivid, joyful vision of your future that you've painted for yourself.

With your this defined goal, you are better equipped to face the challenges of sobriety head-on, knowing that each step you take is a step towards a richer, more fulfilling life. So, let's take this journey together, towards a successful and sustained sobriety with clear goals and a compelling vision.

Taking Full Responsibility

Taking full responsibility means, owning our actions and choices without casting blame on anyone else. This is a crucial step in the journey towards sobriety. Responsibility means knowing that the choices you make, every action you take, affects your path forward. It is about owning up to these choices. Let's explore how it can be done effectively.

First, let's discuss eliminating excuses. Excuses are reasons we give to justify why we haven't met our goals or why we made certain choices. In the context of sobriety, excuses might include blaming stress, social environments, or even friends for our own choice to drink. To take full responsibility, you must stop making these excuses. This is not easy. It requires a strong will and a clear (sober) mind. You need to look at situations plainly and see where your own choices have led you.

How can you start doing this? Begin by reflecting on each day. At the day's end, ask yourself: "What choices did I make today?" Write these down. Look at them. Understand that whatever situation you are in; the choices were yours. This can be a powerful and sometimes painful realization, but it is essential for growth.

Next, embracing ownership of your choices and actions is another fundamental part of taking responsibility. Ownership means when you make a choice, you say, "Yes, I chose this." It's about recognizing your role in your own life without hiding behind others or circumstances. When you own your choices, you control what happens next. This control is empowering. It tells you that if you can lead yourself into a challenge, you can lead yourself out.

But why is this ownership critical in achieving and maintaining sobriety? Because sobriety is not just about avoiding alcohol or drugs. It's about creating a life where you no longer need or want those substances. This can only happen if you are in full control, not just of your actions, but also of your thoughts and reactions. You need to create a strong foundation of self-awareness and self-control. This foundation is built through ownership.

Recognizing the power of personal accountability is an extension of this concept. Personal accountability means being answerable to yourself. It involves setting clear rules for yourself and then ensuring you follow them. Let's say you have decided not to visit a particular place or meet certain people who encourage unhealthy habits. Holding yourself accountable means if you break your own rule, you do not look outward to place the blame. Instead, you look inward. You assess why you made that decision and how you can avoid making the same mistake in the future.

Accountability can also involve others. For instance, telling a friend or a mentor about your goals and having them help you stay on track can be beneficial. However, the primary accountability lies within you. It is your journey, your fight, your responsibility.

To put this into practice, start small. Choose one aspect of your life where you haven't taken full responsibility. It could be as simple as your diet, your exercise routine, or your sleep schedule. Take charge of this one thing. Make better choices and hold yourself accountable for these choices. See how it feels. You'll likely find that taking responsibility in small ways empowers you to handle bigger challenges like maintaining sobriety.

Taking full responsibility is about eliminating excuses, embracing ownership, and recognizing the power of personal accountability. This is your journey. Each step you take is yours to own. When you fully embrace this, you'll find that maintaining sobriety becomes a more attainable goal. You will have developed the strength and resilience needed to face challenges without faltering. Remember, every choice counts, and every action shapes your future. Own them, and you will shape a future where sobriety is your reality.

Now that you understand the importance of taking full

responsibility, let's put these insights into action. Reflect on your choices daily, own them, hold yourself accountable, and start with one small aspect of your life. Build from there. This approach will not only aid in achieving sobriety but will also enhance every area of your life, leading to a fuller, more responsible existence.

Cultivating Discipline and Consistency

When we talk about achieving sobriety, discipline and consistency form the backbone of any successful effort. It's crucial to develop daily habits and routines that reinforce your commitment to sobriety. But what does it really mean to be disciplined and consistent in this context? Let's delve into these concepts deeply and understand their pivotal role in your journey.

Discipline in the realm of sobriety means setting rules for yourself and adhering to them without fail. It requires you to make a firm decision to avoid substances and to stick to this decision every single day. This might sound simple, but it involves a continuous process of making the right choices. Each day, you might face temptations or stressful situations where the easiest choice might seem to revert to old habits. Here, discipline is your tool to remain steadfast on your path.

Consistency is about maintaining your efforts over a long period. It's not just about being sober for a week or a month; it's about integrating sobriety into your lifestyle permanently. This means consistently choosing activities and environments that support your sobriety goals, day after day, without exception. It's about creating a new normal for yourself a lifestyle where sobriety becomes as regular as brushing your teeth.

To foster these key attributes, begin by structuring a daily schedule conducive to your sobriety. This may involve incorporating consistent physical activity and mindfulness practices like meditation and pursuing hobbies that absorb your attention and steer clear of substance-related thoughts. Focus on building a routine reinforcing your commitment to a sober lifestyle through holistic self-care practices. These activities aren't just fillers; they're crucial building blocks that strengthen your mental and physical health, making it easier to maintain sobriety.

Persistence and resilience are also key components of discipline and consistency. There will undoubtedly be challenging days. Days when your resolve is tested, your old habits beckon. It's on these days that your discipline is truly tested, and your consistent adherence to your routine will help you overcome these hurdles. Remember, each time you successfully navigate through a challenging day, your ability to do so again strengthens.

To make this actionable, begin by charting out a daily schedule that includes specific times for sobriety-supporting activities. This schedule should be realistic and should reflect your personal commitments and lifestyle. The key is to follow this schedule diligently. Make it a part of your day, just like eating or sleeping. As days turn into weeks, and weeks into months, you will find that these activities become integral parts of your life, supporting your sobriety without conscious effort.

Additionally, it's crucial to monitor your progress. Keep a journal or use an app to track your adherence to your routine and your feelings and experiences as you navigate your sobriety journey. This tracking can provide valuable insights into what works for you and what doesn't, allowing you to make necessary adjustments to your routine and strategy.

Discipline and consistency in sobriety aren't just about

restricting yourself. They are about creating a new, healthier lifestyle that naturally supports your sobriety goals. By integrating supportive habits and routines into your daily life and sticking to them consistently, you build a strong foundation that fosters long-term sobriety and resilience against challenges. Start small, be realistic, and gradually build your discipline and consistency. Remember, each day is a step towards a healthier, sober life.

By taking these steps, not only will you strengthen your resolve, but you'll also create a life that's fulfilling and rewarding without reliance on substances. This transformational journey is about reclaiming control over your life and shaping it in a way that brings you peace, happiness, and health. Embrace the challenge of discipline and consistency, for they are your allies in achieving and maintaining your sobriety.

Creating a Supportive Environment

When we talk about building a supportive environment, we mean setting up your space both physically and socially to help you stay sober. It's about making sure everything around you helps you keep your commitment to sobriety. This might sound simple, but it plays a huge role in your success.

Consider the people around you first. It's important to be around folks who support your decision to stay sober. These can be friends, family members, or even colleagues who encourage your sobriety. If you surround yourself with people who respect your choice, you'll find it easier to stick to your goals. They won't offer you a drink or urge you to join them in activities where alcohol is central. Instead, they'll help you find other ways to have fun and relax.

Next, think about where you spend a lot of your time. These places should feel safe and shouldn't tempt you to drink. For example, it might help to avoid bars or clubs that focus on alcohol. You might choose to spend more time in coffee shops, parks, or libraries instead. Preferred spaces are those that fill you with peace, not temptations.

Activities are also part of your environment. Choose hobbies and pastimes that don't involve alcohol. Maybe you like painting, hiking, reading, or learning to play the guitar. These activities are not only fun but also keeps your mind off alcohol. When you're enjoying these, you're filling your time with healthy rewarding choices.

What if you encounter triggers that make you want to drink? You will. It's key to know what these are. Triggers may be certain people, places, or even emotions that make you want to drink. Once you are aware of your triggers, you can then consciously work to avoid them. If seeing an old friend who drinks heavily is a trigger, consider seeing them less often. If job or personal stress makes you want to drink, find stress-relief methods that work for you, like yoga or meditation.

Minimizing these triggers in your daily life reduces the risk of slipping up. It's not about avoiding life but about choosing to live it in a way that supports your sobriety goals. You take control of your environment rather than letting it control you.

Thus, creating a supportive environment is about making intentional choices about who you're with, where you go, and what you do. These decisions help you stick to your commitment to stay sober. It's a proactive step in building a lifestyle that supports your sobriety every day. With each choice that aligns with your goals, you reinforce your commitment and make your path to sobriety stronger.

This is just the beginning. Every day, you can make small changes to better support your sobriety. It might not be easy at first, but with time, these choices will become a natural part of your life. You are building a foundation for a sober, healthier, and happier future, one decision at a time.

Every environment you shape to avoid temptation and every positive choice you make takes you one step closer to a sustained sober life. You have the power to shape your surroundings to support your journey. This power is a fundamental tool in your sobriety toolkit.

Keep going. Keep shaping your world. With each supportive friend, with every safe space, and through each healthy activity, you are not only avoiding alcohol but also building a life filled with rewarding sobriety. This is how you turn your commitment into reality.

So, take a moment today to look around. Assess your environment. Are there changes you can make right now? Maybe it's a small adjustment, like deciding to meet a friend in a café instead of a bar. Or perhaps it's time to join a local club or start a new hobby that's been on your mind. Every positive change is a step forward in your sober journey.

Creating a supportive environment is not a one-time task. It's an ongoing process that evolves as you do. As you grow in your sobriety, your needs might change, and so might your environment. Stay flexible and proactive in crafting a space that continues to support your sobriety goals. With this approach, you build not just a safe space but a thriving life in sobriety.

Embracing Failure as Growth

When we think about failure, especially in the context of achieving sobriety, it often carries a heavy, negative weight. However, what if we could change our perspective and see failure not as a setback but as a crucial part of growth? This idea is not just comforting; it is a powerful tool that can significantly transform our journey towards sobriety.

How can you reframe setbacks and relapses? When you're committed to a sober life, any slip-up can feel like a massive defeat. It's easy to get wrapped up in feelings of guilt or shame. However, it's important to understand that growth is rarely a straight path. It involves taking two steps forward and sometimes one step back. This is normal, and it's okay.

Seeing each setback as a lesson instead of a failure can change how you approach your sobriety journey. Think about a time when you learned something important. It likely came from a challenge, not an easy win. Each time you face a setback in your sobriety, you gain insight into what triggers you, what doesn't work, and what you might try next time. This is valuable information that can guide your future decisions.

Embracing this mindset requires practice, and that's where self-compassion comes into play. Being hard on yourself after a relapse is a common reaction, but it's not the most helpful one. Instead, treat yourself with the same kindness and understanding that you would offer a good friend. Acknowledge the difficulty of what you're going through. Remind yourself that perfection is not the goal; continual improvement is.

Maintaining a growth mindset is another key aspect of embracing failure as growth. This means believing that your abilities to achieve sobriety can be developed through dedication and hard work. It's about believing that you can learn from each experience and that each step, no matter how small, is progress. This mindset fuels resilience, making it easier to get back on track after a setback. It helps you to see sobriety not as an all-or-nothing scenario but as a lifelong journey of learning and developing.

Here are some steps to help you implement this approach:

- **Journal about setbacks**: When you experience a setback, write about it. Describe the situation and your feelings, but also try to identify what can be learned. This helps process the event and integrate the lessons.
- **Set small, manageable goals:** After a setback, it's important to regain your confidence. Set small goals that you can achieve quickly. This builds momentum and gets you back on the path to sobriety.
- **Seek feedback:** Talk to someone you trust about your journey. They might offer insights into your setbacks that you hadn't considered.
- **Reflect on progress:** Regularly reflect on how far you have come in your sobriety journey, not just on the setbacks. Celebrate your progress, no matter how small.

By reframing failure as growth, you transform what could be a roadblock into stepping stones. It is a transformational shift in perspective that makes the path to sobriety a journey of continual learning and personal development. Remember, each setback is an opportunity to refine your strategies, understand yourself better, and develop resilience. Embrace each challenge as an essential part of your growth and watch how your journey unfolds with renewed strength and wisdom.

Failure is not the opposite of success in sobriety; it's a part of it. Let this understanding light your path every day. With each step back, you're setting the stage for two leaps forward, armed with better knowledge and a stronger resolve. The journey to sobriety isn't easy, but with the right mindset, each challenge you face is another building block in the foundation of your sober life. So, keep going, keep growing, and remember that every day is a new opportunity to reinforce embracing your commitment to sobriety.

In summary, turning setbacks into growth opportunities is essential for maintaining sobriety. It involves changing your perspective on failure, practicing self-compassion, and adopting a growth mindset. These steps are not just about recovery; they're about building a resilient, fulfilling life. As you continue to apply these principles, you'll find that you're not just surviving without substances; you're thriving in spite of the challenges. So, keep going, keep growing, and remember that every day is a new opportunity to reinforce your commitment to a sober, healthy life.

Chapter 1 Recap

Embracing 100% commitment to sobriety is not just a decision. It is a profound transformation that begins with defining clear sobriety goals and extends to every part of your life, influencing your actions, your environment, and your mindset. Let's take a moment to revisit the key concepts we've covered in this chapter.

Firstly, we discussed the importance of setting your sobriety goal. It's crucial to know what you are aiming for. This isn't just about stopping a behavior; it's about starting a new journey. Goals need to be clear and measurable. Maybe it's not drinking for 30 days, or something personal like improving relationships that alcohol may have damaged. Whatever your milestone, make it specific and write it down.

Next, we moved on to taking full responsibility for your journey. This means no more excuses. You own this path. It's about making a daily decision to stay sober, no matter what life throws your way. Responsibility means recognizing that you are the primary force in your sobriety. This mindset shifts how you handle challenges from a place of victimhood to one of empowerment.

We also covered cultivating discipline and consistency. Sobriety isn't achieved in a day. It's built through daily habits and routines that support your sober life. Whether it's, engaging in regular exercise, or setting aside time for meditation or reflection, these need to be non-negotiable parts of your day. Persistence is your ally here. Even on tough days, sticking to your routines can provide stability and strength.

Crafting a supportive environment is another pillar we explored. This is about surrounding yourself with people who support your sobriety and avoiding places or situations that could trigger a relapse. It might mean making new friends, finding different recreational activities, or even changing your living situation. Every aspect of your environment should reinforce your commitment to sobriety.

Lastly, we discussed embracing failure as a part of growth. Sobriety is a journey that might include setbacks. Relapse, or simply stumbling along the way, doesn't mean the end of your journey; it's a learning opportunity. Self-compassion is vital here. Understand that every setback is a chance to learn and grow stronger.

Now, let's talk about what you can do with this information. Here are some actionable steps to solidify your commitment to sobriety:

- **Write Down Your Sobriety Goals:** Make them specific, measurable, and tied to timelines. For example, "I will not drive by or stop at the bar today"
- **Accept Responsibility:** Each morning, remind yourself that you are in charge of your day and your sobriety. This can be a simple affirmation like, "I am responsible for my sobriety today."
- **Establish Routines:** Create a daily schedule that supports your sobriety. Include time for healthy practices such as exercise, meditation, and hobbies that keep you fulfilled and away from triggers.
- **Assess Your Environment:** Take a look around you. If there are elements or relationships that threaten your sobriety, consider ways to change them. This might mean spending more time with supportive friends or finding new places to spend your leisure time that do not involve alcohol.
- **Learn from Setbacks:** If you face a setback, use it as a learning opportunity. Analyze what went wrong and how you can prevent it in the future. Write these reflections down and discuss them with a mentor or your personal support group.

Each of these steps builds upon the other, forming a solid foundation for your sobriety. Remember, this isn't just about avoiding alcohol or other substances. It's about creating a life where you are actively engaged in activities and relationships that promote your health and happiness. It's about transforming your life and embracing a new identity as someone who is sober, not just someone who is abstaining.

Your journey to sobriety is deeply personal and entirely yours. Each small step you take is a piece of the puzzle in building the sober life you envision. Embrace every part of this journey, cherish your successes, learn from your setbacks, and continually push forward towards a healthier, more fulfilling life. Sobriety is not just a path away from addiction; it's a path towards the life you deserve.

Keep going. You can do this. Every step you take is a step towards victory.

CHAPTER TWO: PILLAR # 2 ANNOUNCE YOUR SOBRIETY GOAL

Setting Measurable Milestones

When you decide to tackle a significant life change like achieving sobriety, it's crucial to set clear and measurable milestones. These milestones act as stepping stones on your path to success. They provide a structured way to monitor your progress and keep your motivation high.

First, let's discuss what a milestone in the context of sobriety might look like. Imagine you've been drinking four beers a day and you want to stop completely. A milestone could be reducing your intake to two beers a day by the end of the month. Another milestone could then be to limit yourself to one beer a day two months later. Eventually, your milestone will be no beers at all. Each of these steps is specific, measurable, and time-bound, making them effective markers of your progress.

Why is setting these milestones important? For one, they break down a large, sometimes intimidating goal into manageable, achievable steps. This can make the task seem less daunting and help prevent feelings of overwhelm. Additionally, achieving these smaller goals can provide a sense of accomplishment. Each time you reach a milestone, you have a tangible proof of your progress, which can be incredibly motivating.

Establishing a timeline for each milestone is equally important. A timeline serves as a deadline that compels action and helps maintain a sense of urgency. Without a timeline, it's easy to let goals slip by or ignore them altogether because there's no sense of 'due date'. For instance, if your goal is to reduce your drinking from four beers a day to no beers, setting a deadline of one month gives you a specific time frame to work within. This helps in planning and adjusting your daily habits to meet this mini-goal.

How do you establish a realistic timeline? Start by evaluating your current habits and behaviors. Be honest about what you think you can achieve in a given time frame. It's important to challenge yourself but also to set realistic expectations that won't lead to disappointment or discourage you. If you're unsure, you might consider consulting with a professional or speaking to others who have achieved sobriety for guidance.

Setting these milestones and timelines requires you to be reflective and introspective, genuinely considering what is achievable for you in your journey. It's about knowing your limits and pushing them just enough to make steady progress. Remember, the journey to sobriety is a marathon, not a sprint. It requires patience, commitment, and most importantly, a plan that you can follow through with consistency and dedication.

In conclusion, breaking your sobriety goal into specific, achievable milestones with established timelines is a powerful strategy. It provides clarity, motivation, and a systematic approach to what can be an overwhelming challenge. By focusing on one small victory at a time, you can gradually build the habits and behaviors necessary for long-term sobriety and health. As you check off each milestone, you not only come closer to your ultimate goal but also build a stronger belief in your ability to commit to and achieve profound life changes.

Remember, each step forward is a part of a bigger journey.

Celebrate your progress, learn from the setbacks, and keep moving towards a healthier, sober you.

Identifying an Accountability Partner

When you decide to set a sobriety goal, one of the most supportive steps you can take is choosing an accountability partner or small group. This person or group plays a critical role by providing you with support and honest feedback throughout your journey. Let's talk about the importance of this choice and how to do it right.

Let's first clarify the concept of an accountability partner. This individual is someone you deeply trust, such as a close friend, family member, or even a professional counselor. Additionally, an accountability partner can extend to a small accountability group, offering collective support and encouragement towards your goals. The key is that they must genuinely care about your well-being and be invested in your success. This relationship is foundational because you will rely on your support system to help keep you motivated, especially during challenging times.

Next, we need to establish clear expectations and boundaries. It's crucial to have an open discussion with your potential accountability partner or group about what you need from them. Do you need them to check in with you daily? Would you prefer a weekly summary of your progress and struggles? Make sure you both agree on how they will provide support. This clarity will prevent misunderstandings and ensure that the support you receive is helpful rather than overwhelming or insufficient.

Choosing the right person or group involves more than picking someone you like; it involves selecting who can be objective and honest with you. They need to be able to tell you the hard truths without worrying about hurting your feelings. This is crucial for your growth and ongoing commitment to sobriety.

Once you have chosen your accountability system, it's important to keep the lines of communication open. Regular conversations about your progress, how you're feeling, and any temptations you might be facing are crucial. These talks can help adjust your strategies to remain on track towards your sobriety goals.

Remember, the role of accountability is not to police you but to empower you. They should offer encouragement and celebrate your victories, no matter how small. This positive reinforcement can make a significant difference in your journey toward long-term sobriety.

In conclusion, selecting and working with an accountability partner or group is a profound step in your sobriety journey. It requires thoughtfulness in choosing the right support system, clear communication to set expectations, and openness to receive and act on feedback. This partnership, when done correctly, can provide you with a much-needed anchor and support system, making your path toward sobriety more achievable and less daunting.

Sharing Your Goals and Commitment

When you decide to share your sobriety goals with people, it marks a significant step in your journey. This is when you move from thinking about sobriety to actively committing to it. Let's talk about what this step involves and why it's helpful.

First, you need to identify your accountability partner. This is the person you trust and feel comfortable discussing your sobriety goals with. Once you've chosen this individual, it's time to share your goals. But what do we mean by 'sharing your goals'? It means clearly stating what you aim to achieve in your sobriety journey. For instance, you might say, "I want to be sober for 30 days." These are examples of specific and measurable goals.

Why is it important to be specific? Because clarity helps both you and your understand what success looks like. Without clear goals, it's hard to measure progress or know when to celebrate achievements. This clarity also gives your accountability partner a clear framework to support you. They know exactly what you're aiming for and can offer specific help and encouragement aligned with your goals.

Expressing your dedication to the process is equally important. This isn't just about stating goals; it's about showing your commitment. When you communicate your dedication, you're telling your accountability partner, "I am serious about this, and I want to make it work." This can be as simple as saying, "I am really committed to these goals and appreciate any support you can offer." This expression of dedication helps to reinforce your own commitment and also helps your accountability partner treat your goals with the seriousness they deserve.

Being open to feedback and guidance is a vital part of this communication. Sobriety isn't easy, and there will be challenges along the way. By telling your accountability partner that you're open to feedback, you're setting up a supportive dialogue. You're saying, "If you see something that I might not see, or if you have advice on how I can handle a situation better, I'm open to hearing it." This openness can lead to valuable insights and advice that might make your sobriety journey smoother and more effective.

Lastly, this process of sharing your goals isn't a one-time

thing. It's an ongoing part of your relationship with your accountability partner. As you progress, your goals might change. Maybe you achieve your initial goals and set new ones, or perhaps you face setbacks and need to adjust your expectations. Regular communication about your goals and commitment helps keep your accountability partner informed and engaged in your journey. It allows them to continue providing relevant and timely support that aligns with your current needs.

In summary, sharing your sobriety goals and commitment with your accountability partner involves clear communication of what you want to achieve and your dedication to achieving it. It includes being open to feedback and willing to engage in an ongoing dialogue about your progress. This step is crucial because it lays the foundation for a supportive and effective accountability relationship, which can significantly enhance your chances of achieving sobriety.

Remember, the journey to sobriety is often challenging, but with clear goals and committed support, it's a journey you don't have to make alone. Your accountability partner can be a pillar of strength and a source of motivation, helping you navigate the path to a sober life.

Establishing Regular Check-ins

When you decide to take control of your sobriety, establishing regular check-ins with your accountability partner is a crucial step. This process involves setting a specific schedule for when you and your partner will meet or communicate to discuss your progress, challenges, and any adjustments needed in your sobriety plan.

The first thing to do is to decide how often you should check in with your partner. This frequency can vary depending on your specific needs and the level of support you require. For some, a weekly check-in might be sufficient, while others might benefit from checking in several times a week. It's important to choose a frequency that ensures you feel supported without feeling overwhelmed.

Next, choose the mode of communication for these check-ins. This could be a face-to-face meeting, a phone call, or even a digital meeting via video calls. The key is to choose a method that makes both you and your accountability partner feel comfortable and facilitates open, honest discussions. If you're someone who finds face-to-face communication more engaging and honest, aim for in-person meetings. However, if schedules or distances don't allow it, video calls can be an effective alternative.

During these check-ins, start by discussing the progress you have made since the last meeting. Highlight any milestones or achievements, no matter how small they may seem. This is crucial for building your confidence and motivation. It's also a time to reflect on what strategies are working for you and which areas might need more attention or a different approach.

Challenges are a natural part of any journey towards sobriety. During your check-ins, openly discuss any challenges or setbacks you've encountered. This discussion should not be seen as a report of failures but as an opportunity to learn and adjust your strategies. Your accountability partner is there to provide support and perhaps offer advice on how to overcome these challenges. Together, you can brainstorm solutions or adjustments to your sobriety plan.

Adjustments to your sobriety plan are sometimes necessary, and regular check-ins provide the perfect opportunity to make these adjustments. Perhaps a certain approach is not working as expected, or you've encountered unexpected triggers. Use your check-ins to reassess and tweak your plan. This could mean setting new, more attainable goals, adjusting your methods for avoiding triggers, or finding new ways to handle stress and anxiety.

It's also beneficial to end each check-in with a brief planning session for the next period until your next meeting. Set a few small, achievable goals based on the discussion you've just had. These goals should be specific, measurable, and tied directly to your larger sobriety goals. By setting these short-term goals, you maintain a clear focus and direction, which can be incredibly motivating.

Remember, the key to effective check-ins is consistency and honesty. Try to stick to the schedule as much as possible. If you need to cancel or reschedule a check-in, do it ahead of time, and always reschedule promptly. This consistency shows commitment to your sobriety journey and respect for your accountability partner's time and effort in helping you.

Lastly, always approach these check-ins with an open mind and a willingness to listen and adapt. Your journey to sobriety is unique, and what works for others might not work for you. Regular check-ins are a tool to help you find your path to a sober life, tailored to your personal needs and circumstances. By being proactive about these regular interactions, you are taking an important step towards maintaining your sobriety and building a supportive relationship that can greatly enhance your ability to stay on track.

In conclusion, establishing regular check-ins with your accountability partner is more than just a routine; it's a fundamental component of your sobriety support system. It allows you to monitor your progress, address challenges timely, and make necessary adjustments to your plan. By actively engaging in this process, you are reinforcing your commitment to sobriety and ensuring that you have the support and resources needed to succeed.

Celebrating Milestone Achievements

When you set a goal, especially one as significant as sobriety, it's important to mark your progress. Celebrating milestone achievements is not just a way of rewarding yourself. It's an integral part of maintaining motivation and reminding yourself of the progress you've made on your journey.

Each milestone you reach on your sobriety pathway is a testament to your commitment, willpower, and hard work. It's a moment of acknowledgment that you're moving in the right direction, and it solidifies your resolve to continue. How you choose to celebrate these moments can have a profound impact on your ongoing commitment to a sober lifestyle.

Firstly, it's crucial to define what constitutes a milestone. This could vary for different people. For some, it might be the first week without a drink; for others, it might be every month or year. The key is consistency and significance. Choose intervals that feel meaningful and challenging yet achievable to you.

Once you've reached a milestone, acknowledging your success is essential. You can do this privately or share it with friends, family, or your accountability partner. Acknowledgement can be as simple as marking the date on a calendar or as elaborate as a small personal ceremony where you reflect on your journey and the efforts you've made.

Celebration doesn't necessarily mean throwing a party. Since the focus is on maintaining a sober lifestyle, consider celebrations that align with your new lifestyle. This could be a day of pampering at a spa, buying a small gift for yourself, a nice meal out, or a movie night. The idea is to choose activities that reinforce your sobriety and do not trigger old habits.

In addition to personal celebrations, consider setting up a reward system. For instance, for every milestone you reach, you could put aside a certain amount of money that you might have otherwise spent on alcohol. This money can then be used to fund a bigger reward once you've reached a longer-term goal. This not only provides motivation but also makes the rewards substantial and satisfying, adding weight to the achievement.

Another way to celebrate milestones could be by engaging in new activities that were not possible while you were drinking. Maybe take a class you've always been interested in or start a new hobby. Engaging in new activities can fill the void that might be left by not drinking and also help build new, healthier routines.

It is also beneficial to share your achievements. Sharing not only helps to hold you accountable but also can inspire others in their sobriety journey. Whether through a blog, social media posts, or speaking at sobriety meetings, letting others know about your milestones can strengthen your personal resolve and encourage others.

Lastly, remember that the journey of sobriety is not linear. There might be setbacks, but each milestone, regardless of when it comes, is a stepping stone towards a lasting change. Every small or big win is a push against the tide of habit and dependence. Celebrate each one with the honor it deserves, and remember that each celebration is a reaffirmation of your commitment to a healthier, sober life.

Therefore, incorporating celebrations into your recovery process is not only fun but strategic. It provides a clear and tangible recognition of your efforts, reinforces your commitment to sobriety, and promotes a healthier lifestyle that supports your long-term goals. Choose celebrations that resonate with your values and support your sobriety, and use these moments as opportunities to reflect on your progress and look forward to the future.

Through these celebrations, you aren't just marking time; you are marking change, growth, and the gradual achievement of a deeply personal goal. They serve as memorable milestones on the map of your new life, each one a story of victory and a step closer to the person you are becoming.

Chapter 2 Recap

When we talk about sobriety, announcing your goal isn't just a step; it's a fundamental part of the journey. This chapter focused on why and how to clearly declare your intention to achieve sobriety. We talked about setting measurable milestones, finding an accountability partner, sharing your goals, establishing regular check-ins, and celebrating milestones. Here, we'll recap these important points and give you steps to make these ideas work for you.

First, setting measurable milestones is crucial. It breaks down your big goal into smaller, more manageable pieces. Think about your final sobriety goal. Now, break it down into smaller goals that you can achieve step by step. For instance, if your goal is to be sober for a year, set the first milestone at one week sober, then one month, three months, and so on. This way, your large goal doesn't seem so daunting.

Next, choose an accountability partner. This should be someone you trust, who will encourage you and hold you accountable without judgment. Sit down with them and explain your goals. Be clear about what you expect from them and ask what they are comfortable with. They might check in with you daily, weekly, or accompany you to meetings. Their role is crucial, so choose wisely.

It's also essential to share your goals and commitment. Don't just think about your goals; speak them out loud. Tell your accountability partner and perhaps others in your support circle about your specific milestones. This not only reinforces your commitment but also lets others know how they can support you.

Establishing regular check-ins is another key element. Decide how often you will meet with your accountability partner to review your progress. These meetings can be in person, over the phone, or even through text messages, whatever works best for you. During these check-ins, be honest about your challenges and achievements. If something isn't working, adjust your plan.

Celebrating milestone achievements often gets overlooked, but it's so important. Each milestone reached is a victory and should be treated as such. Celebrate in ways that support your sobriety. Maybe you treat yourself to a nice dinner, a movie, or a new book. These celebrations not only mark your achievements but also help to motivate you towards the next milestone.

Now, let's put all this into actionable steps:

- **Set Your Milestones:** Write down your ultimate sobriety goal. Underneath, list the smaller milestones you'll aim for along the way. Put dates next to each milestone to track your progress.
- **Select an Accountability Partner:** Think about who in your life would make a good accountability partner. Have a

conversation with them about your goals and what role you'd like them to play.

- **Share Your Commitment:** After you've set your goals and chosen your partner, share these goals with them clearly and specifically. Consider also sharing with a close friend or family member for added support.
- **Schedule Regular Check-Ins:** Decide how often you want to check in with your accountability partner. Schedule these check-ins in advance, whether they're weekly, biweekly, or monthly, and stick to this schedule.
- **Plan Your Celebrations:** Think about appropriate ways to celebrate reaching each milestone. Plan something enjoyable that aligns with your new sober lifestyle.

By following these steps, you are not just dreaming about sobriety; you are actively working towards it. Each step you complete solidifies your commitment and takes you closer to your goal. Remember, the journey to sobriety is a marathon, not a sprint. Take it one step at a time and recognize your progress. You're doing great, and every effort counts.

Always keep the end vision in mind, but focus on one milestone at a time. This approach will make your journey manageable and more successful. In the end, these steps are designed not only to help you achieve sobriety but to build a lifestyle around your new sober self, full of achievements and supported by people who care about your well-being.

CHAPTER THREE: PILLAR # 3 ENGAGE IN DAILY JOURNALING

Starting a Daily Journaling Habit

When you decide to start a daily journaling habit, the first step is simple but vital. You need to choose a dedicated notebook and pen. This choice marks the beginning of your journey. A notebook and a pen are more than just tools; they are your partners in this new habit. The act of picking them out can set the tone for your entire practice. It's best to choose a notebook that feels right in your hands and a pen that flows easily across the page. This makes the process of writing enjoyable and something you look forward to each day.

Once you have your tools, the next step is to establish a consistent time and place for your journaling. Consistency here is key. It helps to turn an action into a habit. Choose a time of day when you are least likely to be disturbed and a place that is quiet and comfortable. This could be early in the morning at your kitchen table or late at night in a cozy corner of your living room. The important thing is that it's a time and place where you can be alone with your thoughts.

The significance of having a dedicated space cannot be overstated. It signals to your brain that it's time to switch into a reflective mode. This space doesn't need to be large or elaborate. It just needs to be yours, a sanctuary where you can pour out your thoughts and feelings without interruption.

Starting a journaling habit also involves committing to it daily. This doesn't mean you need to write pages upon pages each day. Even a few sentences are enough as long as you are consistent. The act of writing regularly is more important than the volume of what you write. It's about training your mind to open up and let thoughts flow. Regularity in journaling offers you a unique opportunity to observe your thoughts and feelings over time, providing insights that sporadic journaling can't.

Why is this daily commitment important? Engaging with your thoughts daily provides a steady stream of self-awareness. You start to notice patterns in your thoughts and behaviors. You become more attuned to your inner life. This can lead to profound discoveries about who you are and what drives you. The routine of daily journaling also instills discipline, a trait that can benefit many other areas of your life.

So, in summary, starting a daily journaling habit requires picking out a dedicated notebook and pen, choosing a consistent time and place, and committing to write each day. These steps, though simple, are foundational. They lay the groundwork for a practice that can significantly enhance your self-awareness and overall mental clarity.

Actionable steps to get started include going to a store today to pick a notebook and pen that feel right to you. Decide on the spot in your home where you will journal and set a daily alert on your phone to remind you of your journaling time. Stick to this routine for at least a month, and observe the changes in your thinking and feeling patterns. Remember, the key here is consistency and commitment to engaging with your thoughts daily.

Journaling is more than just writing down what happened during your day. It is a dialogue with oneself, a method to uncover layers of feelings and ideas that you may not realize in the hustle of daily life. By establishing this practice, you take an essential step towards deeper self-understanding and personal growth.

Writing Freely and Authentically

When we decide to write freely and authentically, we embark on a journey of self-expression that is deeply personal and profoundly liberating. Writing without judgment or self-censorship allows our true thoughts and emotions to surface, which is essential in understanding ourselves better. It's like opening a door to the parts of our minds that we often keep locked away. This process is not just about putting words on a page; it's about discovering who we are from the inside out.

At first, writing authentically might feel strange or uncomfortable. You might find yourself hesitating as you write, worried about what others might think if they read your words. It's important to remember that this space in your journal is yours and yours alone. It's a safe zone where you can express your thoughts and feelings without fear of judgment. The act of writing without self-censorship is a way of telling yourself that your thoughts and feelings are valid and worth exploring.

Why is this process important, especially in the context of sobriety and recovery? In our journey towards recovery, understanding our emotions and thoughts is crucial. It helps us identify what drives our behaviors and allows us to address the root causes of our challenges. By writing freely, we can uncover triggers and patterns that may be contributing to our struggles with sobriety. This insight is invaluable because it provides us with the clarity we need to make positive changes.

How do we begin this process of writing freely and authentically? Start by setting aside a specific time each day for your writing. It doesn't have to be long just a few minutes each day can make a significant difference. During this time, focus solely on letting your thoughts flow. Write quickly, without pausing to correct or edit what you've put down. It's not about crafting perfect sentences; it's about capturing the raw, unfiltered essence of your thoughts and feelings.

Another helpful tip is to keep your writing prompts open-ended. Instead of writing about a specific topic, simply ask yourself at the beginning of each journaling session, "What am I feeling right now?" or "What's on my mind at this moment?" These questions can help guide your writing without boxing you into a specific topic, allowing for more authentic self-expression.

As you continue with this practice, you'll notice that it becomes easier to write freely. The self-censorship that might have held you back at first begins to wane, and your true voice starts to emerge. This is a sign of progress, not just in your writing but in your personal growth as well. Embracing this process helps foster a deeper sense of self-awareness, which is a cornerstone of recovery. You start to understand not just what you do, but why you do it, and this awareness is powerful.

In conclusion, writing freely and authentically is a transformative tool in the journey of recovery. It allows us to explore the depths of our thoughts and emotions, providing insights that are crucial for personal growth and sobriety. This practice helps build a foundation of self-awareness and understanding that supports us in making meaningful changes in our lives. So, take your pen, open your notebook, and allow yourself the freedom to write. It's your journey, your mind, and your story. Write it authentically.

Using Prompts for Self-Reflection

When you begin to use prompts for self-reflection in your daily journaling, you open up new avenues to explore your personal experiences, challenges, and successes. This method is not just about answering questions. It's about delving deeper into your own life and understanding your journey better.

Prompts are designed to guide your thoughts and help you focus on specific aspects of your life that you might not think about regularly. They encourage you to reflect on your progress, express gratitude, and acknowledge the support you have received from others. This process is critical for holistic self-discovery and gaining a better understanding of how you're evolving through your sobriety journey or any other personal growth path.

Why are these prompts so valuable? First, they provide structure. When you sit down with your journal, you might not always know where to start. A prompt can be a starting point that leads you on a path of deeper exploration. For instance, a prompt might ask you to reflect on a moment of joy you experienced this week. This simple question not only encourages you to recall recent positive experiences but also to appreciate the small victories in your daily life.

Another significant aspect of using prompts is their ability to make you think about your challenges and the strategies you used to overcome them. Reflecting on such experiences builds resilience. When you write about how you navigated a difficult situation, you are essentially reminding yourself of your strengths and the support systems you have. This is incredibly empowering, especially on tougher days.

Prompts also encourage gratitude. By regularly noting what you're thankful for, you cultivate a positive mindset that can significantly impact your overall mental health and well-being. Gratitude journaling has been linked to better sleep, fewer symptoms of illness, and more happiness. It's about focusing on the good in your life and recognizing that even in hard times, there is something to be grateful for.

Incorporating guided prompts into your journaling doesn't have to be complex. You can start with simple questions like, "What am I grateful for today?" or "What did I learn this week?" Over time, you can explore more in-depth prompts that ask about life goals, fears, dreams, and reflections on personal growth. The key is to make it a habit a part of your daily routine. This consistency helps you build a rich tapestry of your life's journey, documented in your own words, through your unique perspective.

Let's talk about how to integrate these prompts effectively into your journaling practice. Begin by choosing prompts that resonate with you and your current situation. You might find prompts online, in books, or you could even create your own. Write the prompt at the top of your journal page, and then simply start writing your response. Allow your thoughts to flow freely. This exercise is for you, and there is no right or wrong way to approach it.

As you continue with this practice, review your previous entries regularly. This review process is as crucial as the initial writing. It allows you to see your progress over time, helping you understand patterns in your thoughts and behaviors. You'll begin to notice how your responses to the prompts change, reflecting your personal growth and increased insight.

Lastly, remember that the goal of using prompts is not to reach perfection in self-reflection but to deepen your understanding of yourself and your life's journey. Each entry is a step forward in your path toward personal clarity and recovery. Embrace the process and be patient with yourself as you explore the depths of your thoughts and feelings through journaling.

By consistently using prompts in your journaling, you not only enhance your reflective practices but also reinforce your commitment to your sobriety and personal growth. This method is a powerful tool in your journey, helping you to maintain focus on your goals and appreciate the support system around you. It's a simple, effective way to engage deeply with your inner self, fostering resilience and gratitude along the way.

Recognizing Journaling as Stress Relief

Journaling is more than just writing down thoughts or recording daily events. It acts as a powerful tool to alleviate stress. When we write down our feelings and experiences, it helps us process what is happening in our lives. This process can provide a significant release of emotional tension.

Think about a day when you felt overwhelmed or stressed. Now, consider the relief you might feel by simply sharing those thoughts on paper. This act of expressing oneself is known as expressive writing, and it is a therapeutic practice. By putting thoughts into words, we often give them less power over our emotions. It allows us to step back and evaluate our challenges from a new perspective.

Why is journaling effective for stress relief? Writing helps to slow down your thoughts, giving you a chance to organize and manage them. Imagine your mind as a cluttered desk, with papers all over the place. Journaling helps to file those papers neatly, making everything more manageable. This step-by-step unpacking of thoughts can make the issues you face seem less daunting.

Using journaling to process emotions involves a simple start: just write. Let your thoughts flow without worrying about grammar or style. The key is to transfer your internal experiences onto the paper. If you're angry, scribble it down; if you're anxious, describe that anxiety in as much detail as feels necessary. This act of externalization helps by making your emotions tangible and controllable.

During particularly challenging times, maintaining a journal can serve as a private space to confront fears and frustrations. It becomes a personal retreat where you can be entirely open and honest. For many, this environment is essential for mental health. It's a safe zone where you can express thoughts you might not be ready to share with others.

What should you write about to relieve stress? Start with how you feel. Describe your emotions as clearly as you can. Write about what's bothering you and why. It might also include writing about stressful events that happened during your day, how they affected you, and how you reacted or wished you had reacted. You might see patterns in your responses that you didn't notice before. Recognizing these patterns is the first step in managing your reactions to stress better.

As you continue to use journaling as a stress relief tool, you might want to set aside a specific time each day for this practice. Consistency helps in building a habit, and the regular act of writing can itself become a soothing ritual. By spending this time reflecting on your day and decompressing, you can significantly reduce your overall stress levels.

Remember, the goal of journaling for stress relief is not to keep a log of every minor detail that happens in your day, but rather to focus on those thoughts and events that cause emotional upheaval. By doing so, you're not just documenting your life; you're actively working to manage your emotional well-being.

In conclusion, recognizing the role of journaling in stress relief is crucial for anyone seeking to manage stress effectively. It's a simple, cost-effective method that can be practiced by anyone, anywhere. The act of writing can transform the way you deal with stress, offering both immediate relief and long-term emotional resilience. As you continue on your journey toward sobriety and wellness, consider making journaling a key component of your daily routine. It might just be the tool you need to maintain balance and clarity in your life.

Tracking Personal Progress

When engaging in daily journaling as a part of your journey toward sobriety, it's essential to periodically look back at your journal entries. This practice helps you see how far you have come. It's not just about writing down your thoughts and feelings every day; it's also about understanding the patterns that emerge over time. This understanding can significantly impact your ongoing journey in sobriety.

Let's start with why reviewing your journal entries is so crucial. Each entry you make is like a snapshot of a day in your life. On their own, these entries might seem just like reflections of momentary thoughts or feelings. However, when you look at them together over a period, they begin to tell a story. This story isn't just any story it's your personal narrative of growth, challenges, and victories. You start to see patterns in your behavior, your triggers, and how you cope with stress and cravings. Recognizing these patterns is the first step in mastering control over them.

Now, let's talk about how to review these entries effectively. Set aside a time each month to go through your journal. It could be the last Sunday of the month or any day that you find suitable, as long as it's consistent. As you read, mark entries that stand out because they show a significant emotion, a turning point, or a repeated behavior. You can use simple symbols like a star for breakthroughs or a circle for ongoing struggles. This symbolism will make it easier to spot trends when you skim through your journal later.

What do you do with the trends and patterns you identify? This analysis is your tool for personal growth. For instance, if you notice that you write about feeling anxious mostly on Mondays, you might be stressing about the upcoming work week. With this insight, you can start implementing strategies to cope with this stress, perhaps by preparing for your week every Sunday or engaging in relaxing activities every Monday morning. This proactive approach helps in managing the feelings that might otherwise lead to cravings or relapses.

Celebrating your progress is just as important as identifying patterns. It's easy to be hard on yourself, especially on days when things aren't going as planned. However, your journal will also highlight the many small victories you might overlook. Celebrate these moments. Did you handle a stressful day without resorting to old habits? Write a congratulatory note to yourself in your journal and reflect on the strategies that helped you succeed.

Using insights gained from your journal isn't just about reflection; it's about action. After identifying patterns and celebrating victories, it's essential to use these insights to inform your ongoing sobriety journey. Maybe you've discovered through journaling that spending time outdoors significantly lifts your spirits. Use this insight to plan regular outdoor activities or mini-getaways as part of your sobriety strategy. The goal here is to make your journey as engaging and tailored to your needs as possible, enhancing your chances of long-term success.

Finally, remember that this process of reviewing and learning from your journal is not a one-time task. It's an ongoing part of your journey. As you continue to write and review, you'll find that your entries become more insightful. You'll get better at understanding your thoughts and feelings, and your journal will become an even more powerful tool in your sobriety toolkit.

Every entry you make is a step forward in your journey, and every review session is an opportunity to learn and grow. By tracking your personal progress through journaling, you are not just surviving; you are thriving. This practice empowers you to take control of your life and your sobriety, one page at a time.

Remember, the path to sobriety is a personal journey, and your journal is your map. Keep writing, keep reviewing, and keep growing. Your future self will thank you for the effort you put in today.

Chapter 3 Recap

Let's take a moment to look back at what we've covered about daily journaling. This practice serves as a powerful tool for self-awareness and stress relief. Journaling each day can really change how you understand yourself and manage your feelings, especially on your journey to sobriety.

First, we talked about how to start journaling every day. It begins with something very simple: choosing a dedicated notebook and a pen that feels right in your hand. This is important because your notebook and pen become partners in your journey. You then set a consistent time and place every day to write. This could be in the morning when the house is quiet, or in the evening as a way to unwind. The key is consistency, making it a regular part of your day.

Writing freely and authentically was another important point we discussed. It's all about letting your thoughts and emotions flow onto the page without stopping yourself. This means no worrying about spelling mistakes or what someone else might think. It's just you and your notebook. This process is valuable because it helps you express yourself and discover more about who you are and how you feel.

Using prompts for self-reflection helps guide your thoughts and dig deeper into your personal experiences. Prompts can ask you to think about your challenges, your successes, or what you're grateful for. They help you reflect on your progress and the support system around you. This is crucial for understanding your journey and making plans for the future.

We also recognized journaling as a form of stress relief. Writing down your worries and stresses can feel like unloading a heavy weight. It's cathartic, which means it helps you release emotions and find peace. When you're feeling overwhelmed, turning to your journal can be a very effective strategy to gain clarity and calm your mind.

Finally, tracking your personal progress through journaling involves looking back at your past entries. This lets you see patterns and growth over time. Celebrating your progress is important; it recognizes your efforts and motivates you to continue. Using insights from your journal helps you make informed decisions as you continue your sobriety journey.

Now, here are some specific, actionable steps to incorporate these ideas into your life:

- Pick a quiet corner in your home and declare it your journaling spot. Place your chosen notebook and pen there.
- Set a daily alarm as a reminder to journal. Try to keep this appointment with yourself as you would a doctor's appointment.
- Start each journaling session by writing down how you feel at that moment, no filters. Let everything out on the page.
- Use simple prompts to guide your writing. You could start with questions like, "What am I grateful for today?" or "What did I learn about myself this week?"
- Every month, spend some time reviewing your past entries to observe your emotional growth and patterns. Note any recurring themes or feelings.
- Celebrate small victories. If you notice any positive change or accomplishment, acknowledge it in your journal and perhaps treat yourself to something special.

These steps are designed to help you build a robust journaling practice that supports your sobriety and personal growth. By following these steps, you not only create a valuable habit but also build a deeper understanding of your emotional landscape, which is crucial for long-term recovery and personal well-being. Remember, the act of writing itself is not just about recording life it's a pathway to exploring and affirming life's many layers.

Journaling can transform the way you see yourself and help you navigate the complex journey of sobriety with greater clarity and confidence. Embrace this simple, yet powerful tool and watch as it changes your life, one page at a time.

CHAPTER FOUR: PILLAR # 4 PRACTICE GRATITUDE

Setting Aside Daily Gratitude Time

Gratitude may seem simple to practice, but it holds the power to change our lives, especially when we're on a journey of sobriety. Setting aside a specific time each day to practice gratitude can help you maintain a positive and appreciative mindset. This practice isn't just about giving thanks; it's about deepening your understanding of yourself and your surroundings, enhancing your well-being, and solidifying your commitments to sobriety.

First, let's discuss why it's crucial to establish a dedicated time for gratitude. In the rush of daily life, it's easy to overlook the good moments. By carving out a specific time, you ensure that acknowledging these moments becomes a priority, not an afterthought. This consistency provides a structure that supports emotional stability and resilience. Whether morning, afternoon, or evening, choose a time that suits your schedule and when you can be calm and undistracted.

The next step is choosing a gratitude practice that resonates with you. Everyone is different, and so too should be your approach to gratitude. Some people might find writing in a journal each day helpful. This could involve listing things you are thankful for from the day. Another method could be meditation, focusing on feelings of gratitude, which can deepen your emotional response and enhance your inner peace.

For those who prefer something more interactive, speaking aloud what you are grateful for or discussing it with a friend or family member can be effective. This interaction not only helps to reaffirm these feelings to yourself but also strengthens your relationships with others, creating a support network that is invaluable in sobriety.

Whatever method you choose, make sure it is something that you look forward to doing. This shouldn't be seen as a chore but as a pleasant part of your daily routine. As you continue with this practice, it will become a natural part of your life, just like brushing your teeth or eating breakfast. Over time, this dedicated gratitude time will help to shift your focus from what you lack to what you have, fostering a sense of abundance and contentment.

Remember, the key to a successful gratitude practice is consistency. It's not about the duration of the time spent but about the regularity. Even just a few minutes each day can have profound impacts on your mindset and emotional health. As these moments accumulate, you'll begin to see significant changes not only in your outlook but also in your interactions with others and your overall approach to life.

In conclusion, setting aside a specific time each day for gratitude is a powerful tool in your journey of sobriety. It helps to center your thoughts, appreciate your achievements, and keep your challenges in perspective. By choosing a gratitude practice that suits you and integrating it into your daily routine, you transform what might start as a small task into a profound cornerstone of your daily life. This practice can significantly enhance your emotional and mental health, providing strength and clarity as you continue your path to recovery.

Start today by simply taking a few minutes to reflect on what you are grateful for. You might be surprised by how much there is and how good it makes you feel. Let this be the first step in a journey towards a more fulfilled and grateful existence, supporting not just your sobriety but also your overall happiness and well-being.

Reflecting on Gratitude's Benefits

Gratitude is more than just saying thank you. It's a deeper feeling that can affect your whole life. Let's take a moment to understand what gratitude really does and why it matters so much, especially when you're working on staying sober.

First, let's talk about the emotional benefits. When you focus on what you're thankful for, your mood starts to lift. You might feel lighter or happier inside. This happens because thinking about good things can push away some of the bad feelings. If you're feeling sad or lonely, remembering a good moment or something you're grateful for can be a little like opening the curtains on a sunny day.

Now, imagine this change in mood happening many times. Over time, these little boosts can help you feel less stressed and more calm. That's very important when you're in recovery from addiction. Being able to handle stress well is a big part of staying sober. So, gratitude isn't just nice; it's a powerful tool for keeping your emotions balanced.

Gratitude also has physical benefits. Studies have shown that when people feel grateful, they might take better care of their health. They might choose to eat better, exercise more, or sleep better. All these choices can make your body stronger and healthier. When your body feels good, you're better equipped to handle challenges in sobriety.

But that's not all. Gratitude can make you feel more connected to the world around you. When you appreciate the people in your life, you start to see how much support you have. This can make you feel less alone. It helps you build stronger ties with friends and family who support your sobriety. Also, by showing others that you appreciate them, they are more likely to help you again in the future. This social support is key in recovery.

Professionally, gratitude can help too. When you're grateful, you might see the good in situations more often. This can make you a more positive person to work with. People who are positive and grateful often find more opportunities coming their way. They might get offered more projects or be considered for promotions. This happens because everyone, including bosses and coworkers, likes being around someone who appreciates what they have and what they do.

Finally, let's focus on how gratitude builds a positive mindset and resilience. In recovery, resilience is what helps you get through tough times without falling back into old habits. Each time you choose to focus on what you're grateful for, you're building up a habit of seeing the good in life. This doesn't mean you ignore the bad. Instead, you're training your mind to notice the good while dealing with challenges. This balanced view can make you stronger and more determined to stay sober.

Now that we understand the many benefits of gratitude, we can see why it's such an important practice. It's not just about feeling better in the moment. Gratitude helps you build a foundation of positive emotions, healthier habits, stronger relationships, and a resilient mindset. All these benefits work together to support your journey in sobriety. So, when we talk about gratitude, we're really talking about a key part of your recovery toolkit.

As we move forward, remember that gratitude isn't just something to practice once in a while. The more you make it part of your daily life, the more you'll feel its benefits. So, take a moment each day to reflect on what you're thankful for. Write it down, say it out loud, or just think it quietly. Every bit of gratitude adds up, making you stronger and more ready to face each day with a positive spirit.

Now, why not start right now? Think of one thing you're grateful for today. It could be as simple as a sunny morning, a good cup of coffee, or a message from a friend. Notice how it feels to focus on that good thing. That's the power of gratitude at work, helping you build a happier, healthier life in sobriety.

Keep this practice up, and watch how it transforms your life. You'll find that gratitude isn't just a nice thought; it's a crucial part of your path to long-term sobriety.

Making Gratitude a Daily Habit

Let's explore the important journey of making gratitude a daily habit. It's something simple, yet profoundly impactful. Let's take a moment to delve into how incorporating gratitude into your daily life can transform your routine and enhance your mental and emotional well-being.

First, let's define what it means to make gratitude a daily habit. This involves deliberately finding moments throughout your day to acknowledge and appreciate the good things in your life, no matter how small. This practice is not just about saying 'thank you' casually. It's about deeply feeling and expressing appreciation consistently.

Why is this important? Because gratitude shifts your focus

from what is lacking in your life to what is abundant. This shift in focus can significantly influence your overall perspective and attitude, making you feel more fulfilled and less stressed. For those on a journey of sobriety, these positive feelings are invaluable.

How do you start? Begin by setting a specific time each day dedicated to your gratitude practice. This could be in the morning when you wake up, during lunch, or right before going to bed. The key here is consistency. Choose a time you can stick with so it becomes a natural part of your routine, not an afterthought.

What does this practice look like? It can be as simple as mentally listing three things you are thankful for each day. Alternatively, you might prefer writing them down in a gratitude journal. Some people find it helpful to express their gratitude out loud, either to themselves or to someone else. The method you choose doesn't matter as long as it helps you cultivate a sense of gratitude.

Adapting your gratitude practice to fit your lifestyle is crucial. If you're someone who enjoys technology, there are numerous apps designed to help track and remind you of your gratitude practice. If you're more traditional, a physical journal might be more appealing. The practice should feel refreshing, not burdensome choose a method that resonates with you.

Consistency is the backbone of making gratitude a habit. However, flexibility within that consistency is equally important. If a particular method isn't working for you, it's okay to try something different. The goal is to make the practice of gratitude a seamless part of your life. This means it should integrate into your routine without feeling forced.

As you continue with your gratitude practice, you may start noticing subtle changes in your attitude towards life. Perhaps you'll find yourself smiling more, getting less irritated by small inconveniences, or feeling more connected to the people around you. These changes are signs that your consistent practice of gratitude is beginning to influence your outlook and behavior.

Over time, this daily habit can lead to greater emotional resilience. With gratitude practice, you're essentially training your mind to focus on positivity, which can help buffer against negative emotions and stress. This resilience is particularly beneficial for maintaining sobriety, as it enhances your ability to navigate challenges without turning to substances.

To make gratitude a lasting habit, it's helpful to occasionally reflect on the benefits you're experiencing. Acknowledging that the practice is making a difference in your life can motivate you to continue. Also, consider sharing your gratitude practice with others. Sharing can provide accountability and inspire those around you to adopt a gratitude practice of their own.

Finally, remember that making gratitude a daily habit doesn't mean you ignore the difficulties in your life. It simply means that you're choosing to give your attention and energy to the aspects of your life that you value and appreciate. This choice is powerful and can significantly influence your journey toward sustained sobriety and improved mental health.

In conclusion, incorporating gratitude into your daily routine is a simple, effective strategy to improve your emotional well-being and support your sobriety journey. By choosing a personal and sustainable approach to gratitude, and committing to it consistently, you're setting yourself up for a more joyful, resilient life. So, take these steps today and start transforming your routine into one that actively celebrates and appreciates the abundance in your life.

Taking Responsibility for Your Attitude

When we talk about gratitude, one key aspect often overlooked is the responsibility we have over our own attitudes. You might wonder what this means. It's simple, yet deep. It's about understanding and accepting that you are the one in control of how you respond to different situations and people in your life.

First, let's discuss the importance of avoiding blame. It's easy to blame others or circumstances for our feelings and reactions. However, this approach doesn't empower us. Instead, it makes us feel like victims of situations and other people's actions. Recognizing that you can choose your response helps you move from feeling helpless to feeling empowered.

Now, let's think about what it means to embrace ownership of our choices, reactions, and outlook. Ownership means acknowledging that you have control over your thoughts and feelings. This doesn't mean you won't have automatic reactions to events or that you won't feel emotional pain. What it means is that you recognize you have the power to choose your response after these initial feelings.

Consider this: every moment of the day, you make choices. You decide how to interpret situations, how to feel about others' actions, and what attitude you will carry through the day. When you wake up in the morning, you can choose to be grateful, or you can choose to be displeased about the day ahead. This choice affects your mood, your interactions with others, and ultimately, the course of your day.

The power of gratitude in this process is immense. Gratitude shifts your perspective. It takes your focus from what's missing or wrong to what's present and right. This shift is not just positive thinking; it's a strategy that changes how you perceive and react to life's challenges. By choosing gratitude, you focus on the good in your life, which positively influences your attitude and reactions.

Why is this important in your journey of sobriety? Sobriety is not just about avoiding alcohol or other substances; it's also about building a life where you feel strong, capable, and happy. Gratitude strengthens your emotional resilience. It helps you see the good in challenges and grow from them rather than feeling beaten down.

To start taking responsibility for your attitude, begin each day by deciding to focus on gratitude. Think of three things you are grateful for every morning. They don't have to be big things. Even appreciating a good cup of coffee, the sunshine, or a friend's text message can shift your outlook. This practice sets a positive tone for your day, reminding you that you have good things in your life and the power to choose to focus on them.

Next, throughout the day, observe your reactions. When something bothers you, take a moment to step back. Acknowledge your initial feelings, then consciously decide how you will respond. Ask yourself, "Is there a way to see this differently? Can I find something to be grateful for in this situation?" This doesn't mean denying your feelings but guiding them to help you grow stronger and more positive.

Finally, end your day by reflecting on moments you chose gratitude and how it affected your day. Did it change your interactions? Did it improve your mood? Did it help you handle a difficult situation better? This reflection not only reinforces the power of your choices but also motivates you to continue this practice.

In conclusion, taking responsibility for your attitude through gratitude is a powerful step in enhancing your journey to sobriety. It's about more than feeling good; it's about creating a strong, resilient mindset that propels you forward. Remember, the choice is always yours. Every day, in every moment, you can choose gratitude and shape your life's narrative. It's a simple, yet profound power that lies within you.

Cultivating Gratitude for Growth and Resilience

Gratitude is a powerful tool. It helps us grow and become stronger, especially during tough times. Let's talk about how to use gratitude to help us when we face challenges. This is very important for people who are working on staying sober.

First, we need to understand what gratitude really is. Gratitude means being thankful. It's when we take time to think about all the good things in our lives, even small ones. This could be a sunny day, a friend's smile, or having a home. When we see the good things, we feel happier and more hopeful.

Now, why is this important for growth and resilience? When we face hard times, it's easy to only see the bad things. This can make us feel sad or stuck. But gratitude helps us see the good. This helps us keep going and believe things will get better. It makes us strong inside.

Here's how you can start using gratitude to help you grow and stay strong:

Every day, take a moment to think of three things you are thankful for. Write them down or say them out loud. Doing every day makes it a habit. It gets easier to find things to be thankful for. Even on bad days, you'll start to find small good things.

Next, think about your journey in staying sober. It's not easy. There are good days and bad days. Use gratitude to celebrate your success. Be thankful for your strength to face each day without giving up. This will make you feel proud and strong.

Also, when you face a challenge or a setback, use gratitude to find a lesson. Ask yourself, "What can I learn from this? How can this make me stronger?" This turns a hard time into a helpful lesson. It's a way to grow from each experience.

Another great thing to do is share your gratitude with others. Tell a friend or family member something you are thankful for. This not only makes you feel good but also helps the other person feel good too. Sharing gratitude brings people closer and makes everyone feel more positive.

Lastly, remember that it's okay to have tough days. We all do. On these days, gratitude can be like a light in the dark. It helps us see the good and keep going. It's a tool that makes us stronger, bit by bit, day by day.

In summary, using gratitude each day helps us grow. It makes us see the good in life, learn from challenges, and connect with others. This is especially helpful for anyone working on staying sober. It gives us the strength and hope we need to keep moving forward. So, let's make gratitude a part of our daily life. Let's use it to grow and stay strong. Remember, every bit of gratitude adds up, making a big difference in our journey.

Start today. Find three things to be thankful for. Keep doing it every day. Watch how it changes your view of life and your inner strength. This small habit can lead to big changes. Let gratitude be your tool for growth and resilience in your journey of sobriety.

Keep going, keep growing, and let gratitude guide your way.

Chapter 4 Recap

Gratitude is more than just a feel-good word. It's a powerful tool that can significantly enhance your sobriety and overall well-being. Throughout this chapter, we explored how embedding gratitude into your daily life can shift your outlook and help maintain a positive and resilient mindset.

Let's start by summarizing the key points. First, we discussed setting aside a specific time each day for gratitude. This is crucial as it helps to establish a routine, making gratitude a regular part of your day. Whether you choose to write down what you're thankful for, meditate on positive aspects of your life, or simply list them in your mind, the important part is to make it a consistent practice.

Next, we reflected on the multifaceted benefits of gratitude. Remember, gratitude can improve your emotional state, enhance physical health, enrich your social interactions, and even boost professional outcomes. By focusing on the positive elements, you can foster resilience against daily stresses and challenges in your sobriety journey.

Making gratitude a daily habit is another vital step. Integrating gratitude into your daily routine ensures that it becomes second nature. You can tailor your gratitude practices to fit your personal preferences and lifestyle, thereby making it a seamless part of your daily rhythm.

Additionally, taking responsibility for your attitude plays a pivotal role. By choosing gratitude, you avoid the trap of blame and take ownership of your reactions and outlook. This proactive approach is empowering and can significantly alter your perspective, making sobriety a journey of growth and discovery.

We also emphasized the importance of cultivating gratitude to foster growth and resilience. Gratitude isn't just about being thankful for the good times; it also involves appreciating the challenges and the growth they foster. This mindset can transform obstacles into opportunities, a critical perspective in maintaining sobriety.

Now, let's make these insights actionable. Here are step-by-step guidelines to help you implement the practices discussed:

- **Set a Daily Gratitude Time:** Choose a specific time each day dedicated to gratitude. It could be morning, midday, or evening. Use this time to either write down, think about, or meditate on what you are thankful for.
- **Journal the Benefits:** Keep a gratitude journal where you not only list what you're grateful for but also note any changes in your mood, relationships, and professional life. This will help you see the tangible benefits of your practice.
- **Integrate into Daily Routine:** Find small ways to incorporate gratitude throughout your day. It could be as simple as saying a silent thank you for your meals, acknowledging a colleague's help, or appreciating a pleasant moment of weather.
- **Choose Your Attitude:** Each morning, remind yourself that you have the power to choose your attitude for the day. Decide to approach the day with a sense of thankfulness, regardless of what it may bring.
- **Embrace Challenges as Opportunities:** When faced with difficulties, take a moment to reflect on what the situation can teach you and how it might help you grow. Express gratitude for this growth, even if it's challenging to see in the moment.

By practicing these steps, you can enhance your ability to maintain sobriety with a positive and resilient mindset. Remember, gratitude is a simple but powerful tool that can bring about profound changes in your life. It's not just about feeling better; it's about being better.

In conclusion, embracing gratitude fully and making it a part of your daily life can transform the way you view yourself and the world around you. It's a step towards a more fulfilled and resilient life, crucial for anyone on a sobriety journey who seeks to find strength and positivity in every day.

As you continue to practice gratitude, you'll likely discover more about yourself and how you interact with the world. This self-awareness is a key component of sobriety and personal growth. Keep moving forward, stay grateful, and watch as your life transforms in the most wonderful ways.

CHAPTER FIVE: PILLAR # 5 EMBRACE FORGIVENESS

Understanding Forgiveness as a Personal Choice

Forgiveness is a powerful decision. It's something you choose to do for yourself, not for others. It's about finding peace and moving forward. This choice is crucial, especially when you're on a journey like sobriety, where personal growth and healing are key.

Why is forgiveness a personal choice? It starts with the understanding that holding onto anger and resentment harms you more than anyone else. When someone hurts you, it's natural to feel upset. But if those feelings stay too long, they can make it hard to enjoy life and move on to better things.

Choosing to forgive doesn't mean you're saying what happened was okay. It doesn't mean you forget. Instead, it means you're choosing to let go of the anger that holds you back. This decision is a step toward healing yourself.

It's also important to know that forgiving someone doesn't mean you have to be close to them again. You can forgive someone and still choose to keep your distance. This is especially true if that person hasn't changed their hurtful behavior. Forgiveness is for your emotional freedom. It doesn't require you to rebuild a relationship unless you feel it's right for you.

When you decide to forgive, you do it because it helps you heal. Holding onto pain can keep you stuck. Forgiveness lets you reclaim your power. It allows you to focus on building a happier and healthier life. This choice is a key part of healing and growing, especially in recovery from addiction. Sobriety isn't just about avoiding substances; it's about building a life where you feel whole and at peace.

The act of forgiving can also improve your physical health. Studies show that forgiveness can lead to lower heart rates and blood pressure, which benefits your heart health. It can reduce anxiety and depression, which are common challenges in sobriety. By freeing your mind from negative thoughts, you can find more joy and satisfaction in life.

Making the decision to forgive is a powerful step in your journey. It's not always easy, but it's worth it. It takes strength and courage to let go of pain. But when you do, you open the door to a new chapter in your life. A chapter filled with more peace and freedom.

Remember, forgiveness is a choice that leads to your own healing and growth. It's a personal decision that sets you free from past hurts and opens up new possibilities for happiness in your life. Embrace forgiveness as a part of your recovery and watch how it transforms you from the inside out.

In conclusion, understanding forgiveness as a personal choice helps you regain control of your emotional health. It separates the act of forgiveness from the acts that hurt you. Through forgiveness, you can achieve peace and focus on your sobriety, ensuring a healthier, happier journey ahead.

As you continue to explore this chapter and the techniques in the following sections, remember that forgiveness is a powerful tool in your recovery. It's about more than just saying the words; it's about changing your heart and your life for the better.

Now, let's move forward and explore how confronting painful emotions plays a role in the process of forgiveness, enhancing your ability to heal and grow even further.

Confronting Painful Emotions

Forgiveness is a journey that begins with a single, often difficult step: confronting painful emotions. When you decide to forgive, you are not just saying words. You are starting a process that involves deep, sometimes uncomfortable emotional work. This is essential because it's not just about the other person; it's about your healing and moving forward.

At the heart of this process is vulnerability. It takes a lot of courage to open up and admit that you are hurt. This might seem scary. You might feel like avoiding it. But acknowledging your pain is the first step to healing it. It's like cleaning a wound. It stings at first, but it's necessary for healing.

Why is this important? When you hold onto anger, resentment, or hurt, it's like carrying a heavy weight. It might not seem so bad at first, but over time it gets heavier and heavier until it's all you can feel. By confronting these emotions, you're setting that weight down. You're saying, "This has hurt me, but I choose not to let it control me anymore."

How do you start? First, find a safe space. This could be anywhere that feels secure and comforting. It might be a quiet spot at home, a park, or anywhere you can be alone with your thoughts. Once you're in this space, allow yourself to feel what you're feeling without judgment. It's okay to be angry. It's okay to be sad. These are natural responses to being hurt.

Processing these emotions can take many forms. Some people

find it helpful to write down their feelings. This can be in a journal, a letter that you'll never send, or even a simple note on your phone. The act of writing helps to organize your thoughts and makes your feelings more tangible. It's a way of getting them out of your head and onto paper, which can be incredibly relieving.

For others, talking can be healing. This might be with a trusted friend, a family member, or a professional like a therapist. Speaking about your feelings helps you to hear them out loud and can provide new perspectives. It's also a way to feel supported and understood, which is crucial during this vulnerable time.

Another method is to practice mindfulness or meditation. These practices help you observe your feelings without getting swept away by them. You learn to sit with your emotions, recognize them, and let them go. This can be a powerful tool in managing the intensity of feelings that come with the need to forgive.

Remember, this process is not about rushing to forgive. It's about giving yourself the time and space to heal. You don't need to forgive right away. It's okay to take your time. What's important is that you are honest with yourself about how you feel and that you are taking steps to address those feelings in a healthy way.

As you confront and process your emotions, you might find that your perspective on the situation begins to change. This doesn't mean excusing what was done to you or forgetting about it. Rather, it's about understanding your feelings deeply enough that they no longer hold the same power over you. This is where genuine forgiveness can begin to take root, not forced or rushed, but emerging naturally from a place of real understanding and peace.

In sum, confronting painful emotions is crucial in the path

toward forgiveness. It involves acknowledging and processing those emotions through various means that work best for you, be it writing, talking, or meditating. This step, though challenging, is vital because it leads to a lighter life, free from the burdens of unaddressed hurt. Remember, this is about your healing, your well-being, and ultimately, your peace.

Utilizing Forgiveness Techniques

Finding ways to forgive is not always easy. It's a path that can be both challenging and rewarding. This section discusses some effective methods for facilitating forgiveness. These techniques can help you find peace and move forward. Let's begin by looking at a few practical approaches.

One popular method is writing. You might write a letter to the person who hurt you. This letter is not for sending. It's for you. In this letter, you express all your feelings. You write down everything that hurt you. This process helps by getting those heavy feelings out of your chest and onto paper. It can make the feelings less overwhelming. Writing can be a powerful step towards letting go of pain.

Another technique involves what is called an empty-chair dialogue. This may sound a bit strange at first, but it's quite simple and effective. You imagine the person who hurt you is sitting in an empty chair across from you. You talk to them. You tell them how you feel, what they did, and how it affected you. The key is, you are speaking to an empty chair. This means you can say everything you need to, without worrying about their reaction. It can help you practice what you might want to say to them in real life, or it may help you find closure on your own.

Seeking support is another vital method. This can be from friends, family, or professional counselors. Talking about your feelings with someone else can help you not feel alone. It also gives you a chance to hear a different perspective. Sometimes, others can offer insights or advice that you hadn't considered. Support groups are especially helpful because you meet others who have faced similar issues. Knowing you are not alone in your journey can be very comforting.

Choosing the right technique for you is important. Everyone is different. What works for one person might not work for another. Think about what feels most comfortable to you. Maybe you prefer writing over talking. Maybe you like to deal with things privately, or maybe you find strength in sharing your story with others. Trust your feelings and choose the method that suits your personal preferences and emotional needs.

It's also important to remember that these techniques are tools to help you on your journey to forgiveness. They are not instant solutions. Forgiveness can take time. It's okay if you need to use these methods more than once. Sometimes, emotions can come back, and you might need to go through the process again. This is normal and part of healing.

Finally, remember why you are doing this. Forgiveness is about your peace and healing. It's not about excusing someone else's actions or forgetting what happened. It's about letting go of the hold that the pain has on you. When you work through these techniques, keep your focus on the peace that you are trying to achieve. It's a journey worth taking for your wellbeing and growth.

As you move forward, try to integrate these forgiveness techniques into your routine. Maybe start a journal where you can write letters regularly. Or set aside a quiet time for empty-chair dialogues. Reach out for support when you need it, and be open to the idea of sharing your experiences. With each step, you are moving closer to finding the peace and freedom that comes from forgiveness, an essential pillar in the foundation of sobriety and personal healing.

In conclusion, utilizing forgiveness techniques like writing, empty-chair dialogue, and seeking support can significantly aid your process of forgiving. Remember to choose methods that align with your emotional needs and personal preferences. This choice is crucial in making your journey towards forgiveness not only effective but also a more gentle experience. By addressing and processing your feelings through these techniques, you create space for healing and peace in your life, essential for lasting sobriety and personal growth.

Embracing Forgiveness as a Process

Forgiveness is not something that happens overnight. It is a journey, often a lengthy one, that involves deep introspection, understanding, and patience. Recognizing forgiveness as a process is crucial in managing our expectations and giving ourselves the grace we need to heal properly.

When we first think about forgiving someone, we might feel that once we decide to forgive, our pain and memories will instantly fade away. However, this is seldom the case. Forgiveness can be complex because our emotions are not straightforward. They are woven with our memories, interpretations, and personal values. Therefore, understanding that forgiveness may take time and multiple attempts is vital.

Each time we recall the hurt, we might find ourselves having to decide to forgive again. This does not mean that we have not forgiven or that we are failing at forgiveness. It means we are human, and we are processing complex emotions. It is part of the journey.

Why is it important to see forgiveness as a process? Because it allows us to set realistic expectations about healing. It prevents us from feeling discouraged if negative feelings resurface. It teaches us patience and compassion, not just towards those we are forgiving but also towards ourselves. Forgiving might not come easily. It might require effort each time, like peeling the layers of an onion. Each layer might bring a sting, tears might fall, but progressively, it gets easier to handle.

Forgiveness as a process also involves ongoing practice. You might find some days better than others. Some days, it might feel like the wound has freshly been made, while on other days, it might feel like a scar that has mostly healed over. This fluctuation is perfectly normal.

Practicing patience during this time is essential. We need to be gentle with ourselves and recognize that moving forward takes time. Patience is not passive; it is an active participation in self-healing. It is giving yourself permission to take the time you need to mend your heart at your own pace.

Self-compassion is equally crucial during this process. Be kind to yourself. Speak to yourself like you would to a dear friend in pain. Allow yourself the space to feel hurt, to be angry, or to grieve. These feelings are valid, and they deserve recognition and respect. By practicing self-compassion, we acknowledge our suffering and affirm that it's okay to not be okay as part of the healing process.

How can we apply these concepts practically? Begin by

setting small, manageable expectations for your forgiveness journey. Acknowledge each step forward, no matter how small. Whether it's acknowledging the hurt without falling into old patterns of anger, or recognizing triggers without acting on them, each is a victory.

It might also be helpful to keep a journal of your forgiveness process. Write down moments when you felt you made progress and times when you struggled. This can help you to see the overall progress you are making over time, encouraging you when it feels like you are not moving forward.

Lastly, seek support if you find it hard to cope. Talking to a trusted friend, a counselor, or a support group can make the journey less daunting. They can offer you perspective, support, and encouragement when you need it most.

In conclusion, recognizing and embracing forgiveness as a process helps us to be more patient and compassionate with ourselves as we heal. It allows us to navigate the emotional complexities of forgiveness with a clearer understanding and better tools. While the journey might be long and sometimes difficult, it moves us towards genuine healing and peace.

Forgiving Yourself and Others

Forgiveness is a gentle art that asks us to look at our past, acknowledge our pain, and then, softly, let it go. This can often be easier said than done, especially when the person we need to forgive is ourselves. It's important to understand that forgiving yourself is just as crucial as forgiving others. This section delves into why forgiving ourselves and others plays a pivotal role in our journey toward healing and growth.

When we talk about forgiving ourselves, it means accepting and letting go of our own past mistakes and perceived shortcomings. It's about acknowledging that we are human, capable of errors but also capable of growth and learning. To start, think about a time when you felt you let yourself down. Maybe you made a mistake at work, said something you regret, or simply didn't live up to your own expectations. It's natural to feel disappointment or even harsh self-criticism. However, holding on to these negative feelings ties us to the past and prevents us from moving forward.

To begin the process of self-forgiveness, it's helpful to recognize what happened and why. Take a moment to reflect on the situation. Understand the context and your state of mind at that time. Were there external pressures? Were you under stress? Often, you'll find that you were doing the best you could under the circumstances. Acknowledging this can reduce the harshness of your self-judgment.

Next, look at what the experience taught you. Every mistake is a learning opportunity. Maybe you learned to double-check your work, to think before you speak, or to ask for help when you need it. Recognizing these lessons helps transform regret into a tool for personal growth. Write these lessons down. Seeing them on paper can make them more tangible and easier to remember.

After acknowledging and learning from your mistake, the next step is to actively forgive yourself. This might involve saying it out loud or writing it down. You might say, "I forgive myself for my mistake. I have learned from it, and I am letting it go." This act of self-assurance can be surprisingly powerful. It is a declaration of your intention to move forward with compassion and understanding for yourself.

Similarly, forgiving others who may have caused us pain is essential. This could be as significant as forgiving a betrayal, or as everyday as forgiving a friend who forgot to call. Start by acknowledging the hurt you felt. Understanding that forgiveness does not mean forgetting or excusing the wrong done to you is crucial. It simply means releasing the grip of resentment that can harm your own well-being.

Consider the perspective of the person who wronged you. This isn't about justifying their actions but understanding their human frailty. Maybe they were going through a tough time, or perhaps they didn't understand the impact of their actions. This can soften your feelings of hurt, making it easier to forgive.

Once you're ready, decide to forgive. You might decide to tell the person directly, or you might choose to do it privately within your own heart. The act of deciding to forgive is powerful. It is a conscious choice to release negative emotions that hold you back from peace and happiness. This decision can be liberating, not just for the person forgiven, but for you as well.

Practicing forgiveness, both of ourselves and others, is an ongoing process. It doesn't happen all at once, and that's okay. It's a path that can lead to deeper understanding, compassion, and a more joyful life. Each act of forgiveness, no matter how small, is a step toward a greater peace of mind and heart. So, take your time, be gentle with yourself, and let the process unfold in its own time.

In conclusion, forgiving ourselves and others is a powerful step in our healing process. It allows us to release the past, learn from our experiences, and move forward with greater wisdom and peace. Remember, each moment of forgiveness, whether directed at ourselves or others, adds to our strength and our capacity to embrace life fully. This is the essence of healing, and a powerful foundation for any journey, especially one dedicated to personal growth and sobriety.

As we forgive, we free ourselves from chains of past pains, enabling us to love more freely and live more fully. This is not just about making life easier for ourselves it's about making life richer and more fulfilling. Through forgiveness, we find the pathway to a peace that truly sustains and rejuvenates the soul.

Chapter 5 Recap

Forgiveness is a powerful tool in personal healing and growth, especially during the journey of sobriety. Let's summarize what we've explored in this chapter and provide clear, actionable steps to implement these insights into your life. Forgiveness isn't just about other people; it's also about healing yourself from past hurts and mistakes.

Understanding Forgiveness as a Choice

Firstly, it's crucial to recognize that forgiveness is a choice, not an obligation. This means you decide to let go of grudges for your own well-being, not because someone else deserves it. Deciding to forgive can lead you to experience less anger, bitterness, or upset. It's a decision that can drastically improve your emotional health.

Action Steps:

- Reflect on past events where you've held onto hurt. Write them down.
- Decide which of these you might be ready to start forgiving.
- Commit to the decision by affirming it daily, such as through a morning affirmation.

Confronting Painful Emotions

It takes courage to face your painful emotions rather than pushing them aside. Acknowledging and confronting these feelings is a necessary step towards forgiveness. By dealing with your emotions healthily, you allow yourself to heal and prevent old wounds from influencing your current life negatively.

Action Steps:

- Identify what emotions you feel when recalling hurtful events. Is it anger, sadness, betrayal?
- Express these emotions through a safe outlet, like writing, talking with a friend, or therapy.
- Allow yourself to feel these emotions without judgment, recognizing them as natural responses to betrayal or hurt.

Utilizing Forgiveness Techniques

Various techniques can aid your forgiveness process. Some people find writing letters (that they don't send) to those who've hurt them helpful, while others might use meditation or speak to an empty chair as if the person were there. The key is finding what resonates with you and incorporating it into your routine.

Action Steps:

- Choose a forgiveness technique that feels right for you. Try different methods to find what works best.
- Implement this technique into your daily or weekly routine.
- Be consistent with the practice, even when it feels challenging.

Embracing Forgiveness as a Process

Forgiveness often requires time and repeated effort. It's a process that might need multiple attempts and should be approached with patience and self-compassion. Understand that it's okay if forgiveness doesn't happen immediately or if it needs to be revisited in the future.

Action Steps:

- Acknowledge and accept that forgiveness is a process that might take time.
- Set realistic expectations about your journey toward forgiveness.
- Give yourself grace if progress seems slow or if you have setbacks.

Forgiving Yourself and Others

Forgiveness is not just about others but also forgiving yourself. Extend the same compassion and understanding to yourself for past mistakes and perceived shortcomings. Similarly, try to apply forgiveness to everyday frustrations caused by others, which can help maintain peace and reduce daily stress.

Action Steps:

- Write down things you've done that you find hard to forgive yourself for.
- Reflect on these from a third-person perspective. Would you forgive someone else for these?
- Practice self-forgiveness each day by affirming your worth and accepting your human imperfections.

In conclusion, embracing forgiveness is a powerful step toward healing and growth in your sobriety journey. By understanding forgiveness as a choice, confronting emotions, utilizing techniques, accepting the process, and practicing forgiveness toward yourself and others, you can achieve greater peace and personal growth. Each step you take in this process not only benefits your emotional health but also supports your overall journey in sobriety, aligning with the core ideas of seeking solutions outside traditional methods for maintaining sobriety.

Remember, the path to forgiveness is personal and unique to each individual. It is a journey, not a destination, and every small step forward is a progress towards a healthier, more fulfilled life.

CHAPTER SIX: PILLAR # 6 HARNESS THE POWER OF VISUALIZATION

Determine Your Visualization Goals

First, let's think about visualization. It's like picturing something in your mind. It can be anything you want to get better at or feel better about. Maybe you want to be happier, or you have a big goal you're working towards. Visualization is a tool that can help you get there.

Now, when we talk about setting your visualization goals, we are focusing on what parts of your life you want to work on using this tool. It could be personal growth, reducing stress, or achieving specific goals. It's important to know exactly what you want to improve because this clarity will guide your visualization practice.

So, start by asking yourself, "What do I want to change or enhance in my life?" Think about areas where you feel you could do better or where you want to feel different. This could be your job, your personal relationships, how you handle stress, or even your hobbies.

Once you have identified these areas, the next step is to clarify what you want to achieve. What are the outcomes you desire? This might mean setting a goal to become more confident at work, to handle conflicts in your relationships with more calm, or to feel less anxious in social settings.

Another key aspect of setting your visualization goals involves understanding the emotions you want to experience. How do you want to feel once you've made these improvements? Happy? Peaceful? Empowered? Determined? Visualization not only helps you see the changes but also helps you feel them. This emotional connection can be very powerful in making your visions a reality.

It's also quite useful to write these goals and emotions down. Keeping a record helps you stay focused and remember what you're working towards. It can be as simple as jotting down a few words in a notebook or making a detailed list with steps and timelines. The act of writing helps reinforces your goals in your mind, making your visualization practice more directed and meaningful.

In summary, determining your visualization goals involves identifying the specific areas of your life that you want to improve, clarifying the outcomes you desire, and understanding the emotional states you aim to achieve through your visualization practice. This step is crucial because it sets the foundation for your visualization exercises, ensuring they are focused and effective.

Remember, the clearer and more specific your goals, the more powerful your visualization practice will be. So take your time to really think about what you want to achieve and how you want to feel. This isn't just about seeing a change; it's about creating a vision that motivates and inspires you to make those changes a reality.

Now, with your goals set and your desired outcomes and emotions in mind, you are better equipped to use visualization as a tool to enhance your life. Each visualization session can now be tailored to these objectives, making your practice more targeted and effective. So, keep these goals in mind as you move to the next step of your visualization journey, which involves engaging all your senses to create a vivid, multi-sensory experience.

By taking these steps, you are on your way to transforming your visualization into a powerful catalyst for personal growth and achievement. Keep focusing on your goals, and use your visualization practice to empower yourself towards achieving them. This is how you harness the full potential of visualization, turning your mental images and feelings into real-life changes and successes.

The journey of visualization is unique for everyone, but the key is consistency and clarity. Continue to refine your goals, revisit your desires, and feel the emotions as vividly as you can. This is not just an exercise; it's a transformational practice that can lead you to a more fulfilled and successful life.

Now that you understand how to determine your visualization goals, you are ready to enrich your practice by engaging all your senses, which will be discussed in the next section of this chapter.

Engage All Senses in Your Visualizations

When you begin to practice visualization, it is essential to engage all your senses. This means you don't just see what you want to happen; you also hear it, touch it, taste it, and smell it. Let's go over why this is important and how you can do it.

First, think about something simple, like eating your favorite food. When you remember that experience, you don't just visualize the food, right? You remember how it tastes, how it smells, the texture as you chew it, and the sounds around you while you were eating. Engaging all your senses in your visualization works the same way but for your goals and dreams.

Engaging all your senses makes the visualization more real

and powerful. It's like you are already there, living that moment. This full experience can help your brain believe that this scene is real, which can boost your motivation and confidence.

Here are steps to create vivid, multi-sensory visualizations:

1. **Close your eyes.** Take a few deep breaths to relax. This helps you focus better.
2. **Start with sight**. Picture the scene you want to visualize. Imagine the colors, shapes, and details. For example, if you're visualizing winning a race, see the track, the other runners, the crowd, and the finish line in your mind.
3. **Add in sounds**. What can you hear in this scene? If it's the same race, maybe you hear your footsteps pounding on the track, the cheers of the crowd, and your own breathing.
4. **Next, focus on touch**. In our race example, feel your feet hitting the ground, the texture of your running clothes, and the breeze against your skin as you sprint.
5. **Include taste and smell**. if they apply. Maybe you taste the minty flavor of the gum you are chewing while running, or you smell the fresh grass of the infield and the scent of popcorn from the stands.
6. **Immerse yourself fully**. Feel the emotions tied to this scene. Perhaps you feel a surge of adrenaline, the joy of leading the pack, or the thrill of crossing the finish line. Practice this exercise regularly. The more you practice, the more natural it will become to involve all your senses. Each time, try adding more details and sensations to enrich the experience. These vivid details make the visualization more impactful, helping solidify these images and sensations in your mind.

Remember, the goal of engaging all senses in your visualization is to make the experience as real as possible. This realism can help bridge the gap between where you are now and where you want to be. By vividly imagining that you are already achieving your goals, you're preparing yourself mentally and emotionally to pursue them in the real world.

Through these practices, every session of visualization becomes a powerful rehearsal for real-life action. It's a proactive step in mentally and emotionally setting yourself up for achieving what you truly desire. This method isn't just about seeing a future possibility; it's about creating a whole-body experience that aligns with your deepest aspirations and brings them within reach.

To ensure your success, make it a habit. Set aside a specific time each day for this practice, even if it's just a few minutes. Regular practice strengthens your ability to visualize and helps keep your goals clear and present in your mind, acting as a constant reminder of what you are working towards.

In conclusion, engaging all your senses in visualization is a powerful tool. It transforms a mere mental image into a full-bodied experience, making your goals feel attainable and real. This technique not only prepares you mentally but also aligns your emotions with your objectives, setting a solid foundation for actual achievement. Practice regularly, and watch how it can change the way you approach your dreams and goals.

By turning your visualizations into rich, multi-sensory experiences, you are programming your mind and body to act in ways that lead to success. This is more than just a mental exercise; it is an emotional and bodily engagement that deeply ingrains your goals into your everyday existence, propelling you towards realizing them.

Always remember, the clarity and vividness you bring into your visualization practice can significantly influence your ability to manifest these visions into reality. Keep practicing, keep refining, and keep your senses engaged.

Visualize the Detailed Steps and Positive Emotions

When you start to visualize the steps needed to reach your goals, something powerful happens. You begin to see, in your mind's eye, the path that leads to success. This is not just about dreaming big; it's about creating a clear and actionable roadmap in your mind. Each step you visualize should be detailed. Imagine yourself completing these steps one by one, and each time, achieving a small victory.

Picture this: if your goal is to run a marathon, don't just see the finish line. Instead, visualize yourself waking up early, putting on your running shoes, and heading out for a morning jog. See yourself running through your neighborhood, feeling the cool morning air against your face, and hearing your steady breaths. Each of these moments builds up to the larger goal. By visualizing these details, you're not just dreaming; you're planning.

It's also crucial to tie these visualized steps with positive emotions. Why? Because emotions power our motivations. If you feel good about the steps you're taking, you're more likely to continue taking them. When you visualize, don't just see yourself running; feel the joy of your body growing stronger. Experience the pride in pushing through when you feel like giving up. These emotions will become associated with your activities, making it easier to start and stick with them because they make you feel good.

Now, let's delve deeper into why visualizing these steps and emotions is effective. When you visualize the steps of your journey, you're essentially rehearsing success. This mental rehearsal primes your brain to take the necessary actions in real life. It's like a blueprint; your mind has a plan to follow, which reduces anxiety and increases confidence. The positive emotions you connect to these actions serve as a catalyst, propelling you forward. Feeling happy, proud, or excited about your visualized achievements can boost your real-life efforts.

So, how do you start? Begin by breaking down your goal into manageable steps. If your aim is to improve public speaking, your steps could be researching your topic, writing your speech, practicing in front of a mirror, and finally, delivering the speech in a small group. As you visualize each step, focus intensely on the details what are you saying, how are you standing, what are you feeling? Then, connect positive feelings with each step. Perhaps you feel excited as you find interesting information for your speech, or confident as you perfect your delivery in front of the mirror.

This method can be applied to any goal, whether it's personal development, career advancement, or learning a new skill. The key is consistency. Regular visualization strengthens the mental pathways that help you transform thoughts into actions. For an added layer of effectiveness, you can write down the steps you visualize. This not only reinforces the process but also serves as a quick reference to keep you on track.

In conclusion, visualizing detailed steps and positive emotions is more than just a motivational tool. It is a strategic approach to achieving your goals. By creating a vivid mental image of the steps you need to take, accompanied by positive emotions, you're setting yourself up for real-world success. This technique allows you to experience the journey before it happens, preparing you mentally and emotionally for the road ahead. So, take a moment now, close your eyes, and start visualizing your success. Remember, the clearer the visualization, the closer you are to making it your reality.

By embracing this practice, you're not only working towards your goals but also enhancing your mental and emotional well-being. Each step visualized and each positive emotion felt brings you one step closer to where you want to be. Keep this practice regular and watch as your dreams start turning into your everyday life, step by detailed step.

Practice Visualization Regularly

When you commit to practicing visualization every day, you start to shape your world from the inside out. It's about setting aside a specific time daily for this exercise, just as you would for any other important activity in your life. Just like you brush your teeth every morning, make visualization a non-negotiable part of your daily routine. This consistency is key in transforming your visualizations from mere daydreams into a powerful tool for personal growth.

Each day, pick a quiet spot where you won't be disturbed. This could be early in the morning before others wake up, or late at night when the world is quiet. The goal is to find a time and place where you can relax completely without interruptions. Sit comfortably, close your eyes, and start picturing your goals as vividly as possible. See yourself achieving your dreams, step by step, and immerse yourself in the positive emotions that come with these achievements.

It is also highly beneficial to keep a journal of your visualization practices. After each session, write down what you visualized, including the details of the scenario and the emotions you felt. This practice helps you track your progress and provides insights into the patterns and recurring themes in your visualizations. Perhaps you'll notice certain fears that need addressing, or maybe you'll see clear patterns indicating what truly matters most to you. Over time, you can look back on these entries to see how your focus and goals have evolved. This journal becomes a personal guide and a motivator to continue pushing forward.

Recording your experiences in a journal also adds a layer of accountability. It's a commitment device, reminding you to stay consistent with your visualization practice. On days when it feels tough to get into the right mindset, your journal serves as a reminder of the progress you've made and the emotions that you've felt, reinvigorating your motivation.

While the practice of visualization is a quiet, introspective activity, it can also be helpful to share your experiences with someone you trust. This could be a friend, a family member, or a coach. They can offer support, provide feedback, and help you refine your visualization techniques. Sometimes, saying your goals out loud to another person makes them feel more real and achievable. This social reinforcement can be a powerful motivator.

Another practical tip to enhance your visualization practice is to use reminders. You can set alarms on your phone or stick notes in places you often see, like your bathroom mirror or computer monitor. These reminders should prompt you not only to practice visualization but to maintain a positive mindset throughout the day. They can serve as cues to bring your mind back to your goals, especially during challenging moments.

Visualization is not a one-size-fits-all tool. Feel free to adapt your practice as you learn what works best for you. Maybe you find that visualizing in complete silence is challenging, so you might try listening to calming music or guided visualizations. Perhaps you start by visualizing for five minutes a day, and as you get more comfortable, you gradually increase your time. The key is to make the practice sustainable and enjoyable for you.

Finally, remember that visualization is a skill that gets better with practice. The more regularly you visualize, the clearer and more impactful your visions will become. These mental images will start to influence your subconscious mind, steering your actions and decisions towards making those visions a reality. So, while it might feel a bit awkward or forced at first, with persistence, visualization will become a natural and vital part of your journey towards achieving your goals.

To conclude, the practice of visualization is a potent tool when used consistently. It's about making it a part of your everyday life, documenting the experience, sharing your journey, setting reminders, and continuously refining your approach. Through dedicated practice, you can transform your inner visions into external realities, ultimately leading to significant personal growth and achievement.

Combine Visualization with Focused Effort

Visualization is a powerful tool. It helps us see what we want to achieve. But seeing is only one part of the journey. To make your dreams come true, you need to do more. You need to work hard and keep your focus. This is where combining visualization with effort comes into play.

Think of visualization as planning a trip. You decide where you want to go and what you want to see. But just thinking about it won't get you there. You also need to buy your tickets, pack your bags, and maybe even learn a few words in a new language. It's the same with any goal in life. Visualization is the plan, and effort is the action you take to get there.

Let's break this down into simple steps. First, you use visualization to see your goal. This could be anything. Maybe you want to be better at your job, learn a new skill, or improve your health. Whatever it is, you see it clearly in your mind. You picture your success and how happy it will make you feel.

Now, here comes the important part. You need to move from seeing to doing. This means taking real steps towards your goal. If you want to be better at your job, what actions will help? Maybe you could take a class, ask for feedback from colleagues, or work on a big project. These are the steps that turn your vision into reality.

It's not enough to just start. You have to keep going even when it gets tough. That's where the power of visualization supports your effort. On days when you feel like giving up, remember your vision. Close your eyes and see your success again. This will help you keep your emotional connection to your goal. It reminds you why you started and why you should keep going.

You might wonder how often you should visualize and work towards your goal. It's simple. Make it a part of your daily routine. Spend a few minutes every day picturing your success. Then, take at least one small action towards your goal. Over time, these small steps will add up, and you'll be amazed at how much you've achieved.

Remember, visualization alone won't change your life. It's a tool, but you are the one in control. You hold the power to make your visions real through your actions. Each step you take is a step towards the life you want. Each time you visualize, you strengthen your resolve to keep moving forward. By combining these two powerful strategies, you're not just dreaming. You're doing. That's how you turn your dreams into reality. To sum up, visualize daily, act daily. Keep your goals clear in your mind and take consistent action towards them. This is the key to making the most of visualization and truly transforming your life. You can do it, one step at a time.

Chapter 6 Recap

Let's recap what we've learned about the power of visualization. It's not just about daydreaming or wishing things would happen. It's a focused, deliberate practice that can help you connect deeply with your goals and the steps required to achieve them. Understanding this can transform the way you approach your objectives, making your path to success clearer and more attainable.

First, the practice of visualization allows you to mentally rehearse your desired outcomes. This isn't just about seeing an end result. It's about emotionally connecting with the process and the outcome. When you visualize, you're engaging your mind and emotions, setting a powerful intention that can propel you forward.

To make your visualization practice most effective, you need to start with clear, determined goals. What do you want to achieve? Whether it's personal growth, reducing stress, or reaching a specific goal, clarity is key. This specificity directs your mental energy like a laser, focused on what truly matters to you.

How do you make your visualizations feel real? You engage all your senses. Imagine not only what your goal looks like but also what it sounds like, feels like, even what it might smell and taste like. This multisensory approach anchors the experience in your mind, making it more vivid and real, which enhances its effectiveness.

Visualization also involves picturing the detailed steps involved in reaching your goals and not just the final outcome. This step-by-step approach ensures that you're mentally prepared for the actions you need to take. Moreover, focus on the positive emotions you will experience with each step. Joy, satisfaction, and confidence are all feelings that you can pre-experience through visualization, boosting your motivation and resilience on the journey.

Consistency in practice amplifies the benefits of visualization. By integrating this practice into your daily routine, you solidify its effects. It becomes a part of who you are and how you approach life and challenges. Keeping a journal of your visualization experiences can also enhance this process, giving you a clear record of your emotional and mental landscape over time.

Yet, it's crucial to remember that visualization alone isn't enough. It should be combined with focused effort and actual steps towards your goals. Use visualization to keep your motivation high and your connection to your goals strong, but also stay grounded in the real work it takes to achieve them. This dual approach ensures that your dreams are not just vivid images but are transformed into reality.

So, here are actionable steps you can take today to harness the power of visualization:

- Set clear, specific goals for what you want to achieve through visualization. Write these down in simple terms.
- Begin your visualization practice by engaging all your senses. Picture your goal in as much detail as possible, including sights, sounds, sensations, smells, and tastes.
- Break down your goal into actionable steps. Visualize each step vividly, along with the positive emotions you anticipate feeling as you complete them.
- Make visualization a regular part of your day. Even five minutes daily can have a profound impact.
- Pair your visualization with concrete actions. Create a daily or weekly action plan that moves you toward your goal, inspired by your visualization sessions.
- Keep a journal of your visualization practices. Note your feelings, any changes in your approach, and any insights you gain.

By following these steps, you'll find that visualization is more than just a mental exercise; it becomes a fundamental part of your journey towards personal fulfillment and success. It's a tool that not only prepares you mentally and emotionally but also guides and supports you in the tangible steps toward your dreams.

Remember, the power of visualization lies in its ability to bridge the gap between where you are now and where you want to be. With each session, you're not just imagining the future; you're actively pulling it towards you, making it more attainable. Dive into this practice wholeheartedly, and watch as your life transforms, step by visionary step.

CHAPTER SEVEN: PILLAR # 7 UTILIZE POSITIVE AFFIRMATIONS

Craft Specific Affirmations Aligned with Your Goals

Creating affirmations that are specific, personal, and directly related to your sobriety goals is a powerful tool. Affirmations are short, positive statements that, when repeated often, can help in changing your mindset and your life. They should be crafted carefully to align with what you truly desire to achieve, especially in the realm of sobriety.

Affirmations work best when they are precise. For instance, instead of saying, "I want to be sober," it is more effective to say, "I am living a sober life." This specificity not only clarifies your goals to your subconscious but also helps in reinforcing the idea that these changes are currently happening, which can boost your confidence and determination.

It is also crucial that these affirmations are framed in the present tense. Saying "I will be confident" places confidence in the future, something you are yet to achieve, whereas "I am confident" affirms it as a current trait. This subtle shift in wording can make a significant difference in how you perceive yourself and your capabilities, making the affirmations more powerful and effective.

Why does the present tense work so effectively? It's because our brain doesn't necessarily differentiate between what is happening right now and what we tell it is happening. By stating your affirmations in the present tense, you're conditioning your mind to believe that these traits or achievements are already part of your life. This belief, then, helps to bring about a change in your attitude and actions that can make the affirmation a reality.

This process involves a bit of self-reflection. You need to understand deeply what your personal goals are concerning sobriety. Is it to resist cravings, to be able to attend social events without feeling the urge to drink, or to improve relationships damaged by past behaviors? Once these goals are clear, you can create affirmations that directly support these objectives.

For example, if your goal is to attend social events without drinking, your affirmation could be, "I enjoy social gatherings with a clear mind and a joyful heart." This affirmation supports your sobriety goal by reinforcing the positive aspects of attending social events without relying on alcohol.

Each affirmation you create should resonate with you personally. It should feel right and true when you say it out loud. If it doesn't, it's worth taking the time to adjust it until it does. The personal connection to your affirmation is crucial because it's that connection that gives the affirmation its power to influence your mindset and behavior.

Finally, remember that creating these affirmations is just the beginning. To truly make them effective, they must be repeated often and integrated into your daily life, which will be discussed in the following sections of this chapter. Through consistent use, these affirmations can become a foundational part of your journey to sustained sobriety, acting as reminders and motivators along the way.

In conclusion, crafting specific affirmations aligned with your goals is a vital step in using affirmations to support your sobriety. By making them specific, personal, and stated in the present tense, you enhance their ability to change your mindset and ultimately your behavior. This method can be a powerful tool in maintaining sobriety and leading a healthier, more fulfilling life.

Repeat Affirmations Daily to Reprogram Your Mind

Repeating affirmations daily is a simple yet profound technique to foster positive thinking and self-belief. This method is rooted in the principle that frequent, consistent positive self-statements can reshape our thoughts and eventually, our reality. Including these affirmations into everyday activities like meditation, journaling, or self-reflection enhances their effectiveness.

Let's delve into why repetition is crucial. Consistent affirmation practice plays a significant role in influencing our neural pathways. This is the brain's way of forming and strengthening connections between different pieces of information. When we affirm our aspirations and capabilities regularly, we are essentially telling our brain to pay attention and prioritize these thoughts. This repeated focus gradually alters the pathways in our brains, making the positive thoughts more predominant than any existing negative beliefs.

How does one begin? Firstly, choose a set time and place to recite your affirmations. Many find the early morning, just after waking up, to be an ideal time as the mind is still clear from the night's rest. Others may prefer nighttime, right before sleeping, to reflect on the affirmations and carry them into the subconscious during sleep. The key is consistency. Engaging in this practice daily sets a pattern that the mind comes to expect and accept.

Incorporating affirmations during meditation is particularly powerful. As you sit in silence, repeat your affirmations slowly, matching them with the rhythm of your breath. This synchronicity helps deepen the impact of the words as it ties them with the calming effect of breathing, ingraining the affirmations more deeply into your mind.

Using affirmations while journaling can also be insightful. Write them down as part of your daily entries. Seeing these affirmations in your handwriting makes them more tangible, providing a visual reinforcement of the words. This practice not only reinforces what you are affirming but also encourages you to reflect on them, explore their significance, and perhaps even expand on why these affirmations matter to you personally.

Self-reflection is another enriching way to practice affirmations. This can be as simple as dedicating a few quiet moments in your day to contemplate your affirmations. During this time, think about each affirmation and what it means for your life. Reflect on the changes you hope to see and envision how you will feel when these changes manifest. This mental visualization is a powerful motivator and reinforces the belief in your affirmations.

It is important to remember that the goal of repeating affirmations is not just to say the words but to truly believe them. The belief is what fuels the shift in your mindset and ultimately, your life. As such, it is crucial to choose affirmations that resonate deeply with you and reflect your true desires and values.

Lastly, be patient with the process. Changing thought patterns is a gradual journey. There may be days when you feel like the affirmations are not making a difference. It's natural. Persistence is key. Continue to affirm positively, and slowly, you will start noticing subtle shifts in your thoughts, attitudes, and behaviors. These small changes accumulate over time, leading to significant transformation.

By making affirmations a daily practice, you harness the ability to reshape your thoughts actively. This repeated practice reinforces your ability to direct your thoughts toward your desired outcomes, leading to a powerful shift in your mental and emotional landscape. With each day and each repetition, you are building the foundation for a more positive and empowered life.

Remember, the mind learns through repetition. Make your affirmations daily allies, and watch how they transform your thoughts and your life towards positivity and success in your journey of sobriety.

Integrate Affirmations into Your Lifestyle

Integrating affirmations into your daily life is a powerful step in maintaining a positive mindset and supporting your journey toward sobriety. It involves finding natural opportunities throughout your day to reinforce positive beliefs and replace negative thoughts. Let's explore how you can weave these affirmations into the fabric of your everyday life.

First, consider the times in your day when your mind might be idle or when you are engaged in routine activities. These moments are perfect for practicing affirmations. For example, while commuting to work or school, instead of letting your mind wander into possibly stressful or unproductive thoughts, you can repeat affirmations. Say them out loud or in your head. Phrases like "I am in control" or "Today, I choose my happiness" can set a positive tone for the day ahead.

Similarly, during exercise, whether it's a morning jog, a quick midday walk, or an evening workout session, affirmations can be a motivational companion. As your body moves and you create energy, affirm your strength and resolve. You might say, "I am stronger with each step I take" or "I am committed to my health and well-being." This practice not only strengthens the body but also fortifies the mind.

Another practical way to integrate affirmations into your lifestyle is by replacing negative self-talk as it arises. We often don't realize when we slip into patterns of self-criticism or doubt. By having a set of go-to affirmations, you can consciously counteract these thoughts. When you catch yourself thinking, "I can't do this," quickly replace it with, "I am capable and strong." This switch in dialogue can drastically alter your emotional and mental state, promoting a more positive outlook on life.

It's also beneficial to use affirmations during times of stress or when facing challenges. They serve as reminders of your abilities and goals, and help focus your mind on positive outcomes. For instance, before a stressful meeting or during a tough conversation, remind yourself, "I handle my challenges with grace and ease," or "I am calm and prepared for any situation." These affirmations help in maintaining composure and confidence in challenging times.

To make this practice even more effective, you can set reminders on your phone or post notes in places you often look, like on your bathroom mirror or the dashboard of your car. These visual cues can prompt you to repeat your affirmations, thus embedding them deeper into your consciousness. Over time, this practice helps in shifting your mental patterns and reinforcing a positive self-image, which is crucial for anyone committed to sobriety and personal growth.

Incorporating affirmations into your lifestyle doesn't require extra time or resources; it simply involves a shift in awareness and the deliberate use of positive language throughout your day. By doing this, you transform ordinary moments into opportunities for personal development and reinforce your commitment to sobriety and well-being.

Remember, the key to making affirmations work is consistency. Make them a part of your daily routine, and soon, they will become a natural part of your thought process, supporting you in your journey toward a healthier, more positive life. Affirmations are not just words; they are declarations of your reality and intentions. Use them wisely and watch as they transform not only your thoughts but also your actions and reactions to the world around you.

Make Affirmations Vivid and Emotion-Evoking

When we talk about making affirmations vivid and full of emotion, it means crafting statements that not only state a desire or a goal but do so in a way that paints a clear and compelling picture in your mind. Think about the difference between a simple, flat statement and one that bursts with color, detail, and life. The more vivid your affirmation, the more likely it is to impact your feelings and, ultimately, your reality.

Affirmations are powerful tools. They help to reshape your thinking and can even alter the way you view yourself and your environment. But for affirmations to truly work, they need to do more than just repeat words; they must stir emotions and spark the imagination.

Let's start by exploring how to make your affirmations vivid. To do this, you will want to use descriptive language. Instead of saying, "I am confident," you might say, "I feel a warm, steady confidence radiating through me in every situation." Notice how the second statement creates a more dynamic image and sensation. It's not just about being confident; it's about experiencing that confidence in a tangible way.

Descriptive language engages your senses, making your affirmation more relatable and real. Imagine you are trying to build confidence in public speaking. A vivid affirmation could be, "I stand on stage, feeling a comforting cool breeze as I confidently share my thoughts with a smiling, attentive audience." This affirmation does more than proclaim confidence it pulls you into the scenario, letting you experience the moment with sights, sounds, and sensations.

Now, let's discuss infusing your affirmations with positive emotions. Emotions are the language of the subconscious mind. When you tie strong, positive emotions to your affirmations, you enhance their ability to reshape your thoughts and beliefs. It's like planting a seed in fertile soil it grows stronger and faster.

If your goal is to feel happier every day, you might use an affirmation like, "I embrace each day with joy and laughter, feeling the happiness bubble up inside me with every breath I take." This affirmation does not just state that you are happy; it makes you feel the joy with its words.

The key to successful emotional affirmations is to focus on the feeling you wish to cultivate. Before you craft your affirmation, take a moment to really feel the emotion you want to embed. Where do you feel it in your body? What does it remind you of?

Once you have a clear sense of the emotion, weave it into your affirmation.

Incorporating gratitude is another powerful way to charge your affirmations with emotion. Gratitude naturally elevates your mood and can help shift your focus from what you lack to what you have. An affirmation infused with gratitude might look like this: "I am deeply grateful for my ability to learn and grow, which brings new opportunities to my life every day." This not only affirms your growth but also celebrates it, making you feel more appreciative and open to new possibilities.

By making your affirmations vivid and emotionally charged, they become much more than just words. They transform into experiences, feelings, and visions that can effectively reprogram your mind towards greater positivity and resilience. This technique is especially potent when using affirmations to support sobriety, as it reinforces your commitment to a healthier, happier life every time you recall or recite your affirmations.

To practice, choose one area in your life you wish to improve with affirmations. Craft a vivid, emotionally rich statement that reflects your desired outcome. Repeat this affirmation daily, ideally in a calm and relaxed state, and observe the changes in your feelings and beliefs over time. Remember, consistency is key. The repeated emotional and sensory engagement will help solidify these new, positive neural pathways, gradually making them your new reality.

In closing, vivid and emotion-evoking affirmations are not just helpful; they are transformative. They provide a multi-sensory experience that engages both mind and heart, anchoring positive beliefs deeply into your subconscious. With regular practice, these affirmations will not only support your sobriety but also enhance your overall quality of life, making you feel more empowered and aligned with your true self.

Keep your affirmations clear, vivid, and emotionally enriching, and watch as they bring about meaningful and lasting change in your journey toward sobriety and beyond.

Use Affirmations to Support Visualization

When we talk about using affirmations in combination with visualization, we are exploring a powerful method to enhance our mental landscape. Visualization is the practice of imagining what you want to achieve in vivid detail as if it is already happening. It's like creating a mental movie where you are the director and the star. This technique is often used by athletes, entrepreneurs, and artists to improve performance, motivation, and confidence.

Now, let's bring affirmations into this mix. Affirmations are positive, specific statements that help you to overcome negative thoughts. They are crafted to reflect the reality you wish to create and are phrased in the present tense. Imagine you are using a tool that helps plant flowers in your garden. In this scenario, affirmations are the seeds you're planting in the soil of your mind, and visualization is the sunlight and water that help these seeds to grow and bloom.

The first step is to create affirmations that align closely with the visions you have of your success. For instance, if your goal is to maintain sobriety, your affirmation might be, "I am living a healthy and vibrant life free from alcohol." This affirmation should be repeated regularly, each time you say it, try to really feel and believe in the words.

Next, when you settle down to visualize, start by finding a

quiet space where you won't be disturbed. Close your eyes and begin by taking a few deep breaths to relax your mind and body. Now, start imagining the scenario where you are living that affirmation. See yourself turning down offers of alcohol effortlessly, engaging in healthy activities, and feeling happier. Make your mental imagery as detailed as possible picture where you are, who you are with, what you are doing, even what you are wearing. Use your affirmation as a soundtrack to this mental movie.

This practice combines the power of both techniques. While affirmations align your thoughts for success, visualization energizes your emotions and senses, making the experience more powerful. Each time you practice, you are essentially rehearsing success. This not only helps to strengthen your belief that you can achieve your goals but also primes your brain to seize opportunities that make these goals a reality.

It's important to practice consistently. Integration of affirmations with visualization should become a regular part of your routine, perhaps each morning or before you go to sleep at night. Over time, this practice will help in rewiring your brain's neural pathways, making it naturally inclined to think positively and stay motivated towards maintaining sobriety or any other goal you've set for yourself.

The beauty of affirmations and visualization is that they empower you to take control of your thoughts and emotions. They transform passive hopes into active beliefs, pushing you towards your goals. The more vividly you can imagine your success and the more passionately you can affirm it, the more real and achievable it will seem. So, take this tool and use it daily as a way to nurture and grow the reality you want to live in. Remember, your mind is a powerful ally in your journey towards personal growth and sobriety.

Chapter 7 Recap

By now, you've learned a lot about the power of positive affirmations in your journey toward sobriety. The importance of these affirmations cannot be overstressed. They are more than just positive statements; they are tools that reshape your thinking and strengthen your belief in your ability to maintain sobriety. This chapter has guided you through different ways to craft, use, and integrate affirmations into your daily life. Let's recap the essential steps and strategies you should carry forward.

First, creating specific affirmations that resonate with your personal sobriety goals is crucial. These affirmations should be precise. They are not just hopeful thoughts but are affirmations crafted in the present tense. For instance, instead of saying, "I will be sober," affirm "I am living a sober life." This small shift in wording reinforces the belief that you are currently achieving what you're affirming, making it a present reality rather than a distant goal.

Next, repetition plays a critical role in embedding these affirmations into your subconscious. Daily repetition transforms these affirmations from mere words to integral beliefs that guide your actions and reactions. Whether you choose to repeat these affirmations during quiet morning reflections, or while journaling in the evening, consistency is key. Every repetition is a step towards rewiring your brain's pathways, replacing old, destructive beliefs with new, supportive ones.

Incorporating affirmations into your lifestyle means you

integrate them into your daily routines. It involves saying them during different activities, like while you're commuting to work or during your exercise sessions. This integration ensures that your affirmations are not just part of your morning routine but are woven throughout your daily life, continuously working to uplift and support your sobriety.

Making your affirmations vivid and emotionally charged can significantly enhance their impact. Instead of a simple, "I am sober," enrich your affirmations with details that engage your senses and evoke positive emotions. A more powerful affirmation could be, "I feel vibrant and full of energy living a sober life." By engaging your emotions, you connect more deeply with your affirmations, giving them the power to more effectively influence your subconscious mind.

Lastly, affirmations can be combined with visualization techniques to multiply their effects. Visualization is not merely about seeing the change you want it's about feeling and experiencing the change in your mind's eye as if it's already happened. When you visualize your sobriety, incorporate your affirmations to reinforce the visualized outcomes, making the mental imagery stronger and more compelling.

Here are some actionable steps you can follow:

- Craft at least three specific affirmations related to your sobriety goals. Write them in the present tense.
- Set aside two specific times each day to repeat your affirmations. Perhaps once in the morning and once at night.
- Find moments throughout your day when you can repeat these affirmations. It could be when you're washing dishes or taking a shower.
- Each time you say an affirmation, try to really feel its truth.

Make it vivid. Imagine the joy, the freedom, or the peace that comes with sobriety.

- Once a week, spend a few minutes visualizing your life as a sober individual. See yourself turning down drinks at a party, waking up feeling fresh, or enjoying activities that don't involve alcohol. Use your affirmations to guide this visualization.

Implementing these steps will help you make affirmations a powerful tool in maintaining sobriety. They reinforce the positive beliefs about yourself and your life, supporting you in your journey towards a healthier, sober lifestyle. Remember, the goal of affirmations is not just to speak something into existence but to believe it so deeply that it becomes your reality. With continuous practice, these affirmations will become an integral part of your thought process, empowering you to remain sober.

Every step you take in this process is a step towards a stronger, more resilient you. By effectively using affirmations, you not only support your journey of sobriety but also enhance your overall wellbeing and outlook on life. Keep moving forward, keep affirming, and let each day bring you closer to the sober life you aspire to live.

Through these methods, you solidify the foundation of your sobriety, built upon the powerful tool of positive affirmations. Each affirmation is a brick in the fortress protecting your decision to live soberly. Remember, your words have power use them to shape a sober, fulfilling life.

CHAPTER EIGHT: BUILD YOUR PERSONAL SUPPORT SYSTEM

Identify Supportive Relationships

When we talk about building a strong foundation for sobriety, one of the first steps is to identify supportive relationships. This means taking a close look at the people around us and deciding who truly supports our journey to stay sober. It's about finding those who not only respect our decision but also actively encourage and uplift us.

Let's start by evaluating your existing relationships. Think about the people you spend most of your time with. Do they support your goals? Are they positive influences who encourage you to be your best self? It's crucial to surround yourself with individuals who make you feel safe, respected, and valued. These are the people who will not tempt you with substances or behaviors that conflict with your sobriety. Instead, they will help you focus on your growth and recovery.

To identify these supportive individuals, consider how you feel after you spend time with them. Do you feel energized and positive, or do you feel drained and negative? Those who contribute to your feelings of positivity are likely good candidates for your support system. It's important to have friends who listen to you, offer help when needed, and share your commitment to sobriety.

While assessing your current relationships, it's equally

important to seek out new connections. Look for groups and communities that align with your values. This could be a local or online sobriety support group, a hobby club where alcohol or drugs are not the focus, or a volunteer organization that promotes healthy living. Meeting new people who share your commitment to sobriety can provide additional layers of support and motivation.

Creating supportive relationships is not just about having people around. It's about having the right people around. Those who understand your journey and are there to back you up without judgment. This network of supporters plays a crucial role in your sobriety by offering encouragement and understanding when you need it most. They are your allies in your commitment to a sober and healthier lifestyle.

In conclusion, building a personal support system is essential for anyone committed to maintaining sobriety. Start by evaluating your current relationships, identifying those who truly support your sobriety goals, and then seek out new, like-minded individuals. By surrounding yourself with positive influences, you construct a supportive environment that fosters personal growth and helps maintain your sobriety. Remember, the right relationships can make all the difference in your journey to a healthier, sober life.

Having supportive relationships is more than just feeling good. It's about creating a stable, positive environment that consistently nurtures your decision to live soberly. This foundation not only supports your current state but also bolsters your resilience against future challenges. It's a proactive step towards a sustained, fulfilling sobriety.

Foster Honest and Open Communication

Building a strong support system is vital for anyone, especially for those on a journey toward sobriety. One of the most critical steps in this process is fostering honest and open communication with people who support you. This means being real about your feelings, your struggles, and your successes. It's about creating a space where everyone feels safe to express themselves without fear of judgment.

Let's start by discussing what it means to practice vulnerability. Being vulnerable involves showing your true self. It means sharing not just the good parts of your life but also the challenges you face. This can be hard. You might worry that people will see you differently or that they might treat you with less respect. The truth is, showing your real, full self can strengthen your relationships. It makes people feel closer to you and shows them that you trust them.

Next, think about authenticity. This is all about being yourself. It means not hiding who you are or pretending to be something you're not. It's important because it builds trust. When people know you are being genuine, they are more likely to be genuine in return. This trust is a cornerstone of any strong relationship.

Now, how do you put this into practice? Start small. Choose one person in your support system whom you trust deeply. Share something with them that you haven't shared before. It could be a feeling you've been holding back, a fear about your sobriety journey, or even a small success you've had recently. When you share, pay attention to how they respond. If they support you without judgment, it's a good sign that you can open up more in the future.

Encouraging open and non-judgmental communication is the next step. This means creating a space where everyone feels they can speak freely. You can do this by always responding with kindness and understanding, even when you don't fully agree with what someone is saying. Show appreciation for their honesty, and resist the urge to offer quick fixes. Sometimes, just listening is more helpful than offering solutions.

Creating a sense of communion within your support group is also essential. Communion here means a deep sense of sharing and understanding. It's the feeling that you are all in this together. Celebrate each other's milestones, and be there for each other during setbacks. This shared journey can make your bonds stronger and give everyone involved a deeper sense of purpose and connection.

It's important to remember that building this kind of communication takes time. It doesn't happen overnight. But each step you take towards being more open and supportive helps create a stronger, more supportive environment. This environment is not just beneficial for you but for everyone in your support circle. It fosters growth, healing, and a deeper understanding of each other.

In conclusion, fostering honest and open communication within your support system is crucial for your sobriety journey. It enhances trust, builds stronger relationships, and creates a supportive network that can help you through tough times. Start by being vulnerable and authentic with one person, encourage open dialogue, and gradually expand these practices within your group. With patience and persistence, you will see your support system strengthen, giving you a greater foundation in your journey toward sobriety.

Remember, every step you take in building honest communication helps not only you but also those around you, making your collective journey towards growth and sobriety a shared and supportive experience.

Remove Negative Influences

When you are working hard at staying sober, it's crucial to look at the people around you. Some friends or even family members might not support your journey. They may even make it harder for you to stay on track. You need to know who these people are.

First, think about your relationships. Who makes you feel good about your sobriety? Who doesn't? It might be tough, but it's important to be honest with yourself. If someone is making it harder for you to stay sober, you need to address it.

Setting clear boundaries is your next step. This means you tell people what is okay and what is not okay. For example, you can say, "I am not comfortable being around alcohol right now." If they care about you, they will understand and support your choice.

Sometimes, setting boundaries might not be enough. Some people might still make things difficult for you. In these cases, distancing yourself might be necessary. This can be hard, especially if you care about them. But your sobriety is very important, and you need to put yourself first.

You might worry about how these changes will affect your relationships. That's normal. Remember, it's okay to seek help. You can talk to a counselor or a trusted friend about how to handle these situations. They can give you advice and support.

Removing negative influences is about making sure that the people in your life support your sobriety. When you have the right support, staying sober is much easier. You deserve to be surrounded by people who help you feel strong and confident in your sobriety.

Lastly, remember this is a process. Deciding who supports your sobriety and setting boundaries can take time. It's okay to take small steps. What's important is that you're moving forward and making the best choices for your sobriety.

By following these steps, you are building a stronger foundation for your sober life. This is a big part of success in staying sober. You are doing great by making these tough choices and sticking to them.

Always remember you're not alone in this. Many others are also working hard at sobriety. They, too, have had to make tough decisions about the people in their lives. Like them, you have the strength to make these decisions and keep moving forward on your path to a healthier, sober life.

Every step you take to remove negative influences is a step towards a stronger, more secure you. Keep going. You can do this. Your sobriety is worth it. And so are you.

Pay Attention to Environmental Influences

When we talk about our journey towards sobriety and personal growth, we often focus on our internal struggles and achievements. However, the environment we find ourselves in plays a significant role in shaping our thoughts and actions. It's crucial to be aware of this as we aim to support our sobriety goals.

What do we mean by environmental influences? It's the attitudes, beliefs, and behaviors of the people around us. These can affect us deeply, often in ways we might not immediately notice.

For example, if you spend time with friends who often drink

heavily, you might find it harder to stick to your sobriety. Their behavior might make drinking seem normal and okay, even when it's not what you want for yourself. On the other hand, if you are around people who prioritize healthy habits, you might find it easier to do the same.

The first step to managing environmental influences is to become very aware of them. Start noticing what behaviors or attitudes make you feel good and which ones don't. This awareness is powerful. It can help you make better choices about who you spend your time with.

Once you know the influences around you, try to surround yourself with people who have the qualities you admire and wish to develop. Look for friends who are kind, patient, or whatever traits you value. These people can act as role models. You can learn from them just by being around them.

It's important to remember that you don't need to cut off everyone who doesn't fit your ideal. But you can choose to spend more time with those who support your goals. This choice can make a big difference in your journey.

Creating a personal environment that reflects your values isn't just about being selective with your social circle. It also involves participating in activities that align with your goals. If sobriety is your aim, engage in sober activities. Maybe you can join a sports team, take up a new hobby like painting or join a book club. All of these can help you meet new people who are also living sober lives.

Moreover, remember that everyone has moments of weakness. When you find yourself in a challenging environment, have a plan ready. This could be a simple reminder on your phone that lists the reasons you chose sobriety or having a supportive friend to call.

These small preparations can help you stay strong in moments of temptation.

It is also helpful to regularly reflect on your progress and adjust your environment as needed. Maybe a friend who initially supported your sobriety has started to influence you negatively. It's okay to reassess and make changes to your social circle. This doesn't mean you care about them any less; it just means you are prioritizing your health and goals.

In conclusion, paying attention to the environmental influences around you is a crucial step in supporting your sobriety journey. By being aware of these influences, actively choosing positive environments, and having plans in place for difficult situations, you empower yourself to maintain the lifestyle you desire. Surround yourself with people and activities that uplift you, and you'll find it easier to stick to your path of sobriety and personal growth.

Remember, every choice about who you spend time with or what activities you engage in is shaping your future. Make these choices wisely, and watch how they help you build a life that aligns with your sobriety goals.

By mastering your environment, you master your decisions and your life. Let's continue to make choices that support our journey to a healthier, happier self.

This section of the book not only guides you in assessing your surroundings but also empowers you to make changes that align with your personal growth and sobriety. By understanding and adjusting your environmental influences, you are taking an active role in your recovery and ensuring that you are surrounded by positivity and support. This proactive approach is a key pillar in the foundation of a sober and fulfilling life.

Shape Your Physical Environment

Let's talk about shaping your physical environment to support your sobriety goals. This is crucial because our surroundings can influence our behaviors and choices deeply. The space around you should help you feel safe, peaceful, and motivated, not remind you of past habits you are trying to change.

First, think about where you spend most of your time. This might be your home or perhaps a specific room in your home. Look around. What do you see? If there are items that remind you of times when you were drinking or using substances, it is a good idea to remove them. This could be bottles, glasses, or anything else directly connected to your past habits.

Instead, fill your space with things that help you feel positive and calm. This could be inspiring artwork or photos of loved ones who support your journey to sobriety. These visuals should serve as reminders of your commitment and the supportive network around you.

Next, consider adding elements that promote relaxation and focus. This might include plants, which not only beautify a space but also improve air quality, or a small fountain that adds soothing background noise. Such details can enhance the tranquility of your environment, making it a place where you can thrive without stress triggers.

Lighting is another important aspect. Bright, harsh lighting can make it difficult to relax, so opt for softer, warmer lighting. This can make your space feel cozier and less clinical. On the other hand, ensure there is enough light for you to read or engage in hobbies that keep your mind occupied and away from thoughts of drinking or using drugs.

Organization plays a vital role as well. A cluttered space can lead to a cluttered mind, which might make it harder to stick to your sobriety goals. By keeping your environment tidy and organized, you create a sense of order and control. This can be incredibly empowering, especially on difficult days.

Don't underestimate the power of color, either. Colors can greatly affect our mood and thoughts. Consider repainting your walls with colors that evoke peace and calmness, such as soft blues, greens, or earth tones. These colors can help create a serene atmosphere that supports your mental and emotional well-being.

Finally, designate areas in your home for specific activities. Have a clear area for relaxation, another for work or study, and a separate one for physical activities like yoga or exercise. This helps in creating a balanced life, where you have a structured routine that supports your sobriety. Each area serves as a cue for the activity that should happen there, which helps in maintaining a disciplined lifestyle.

Remember that shaping your physical environment is a continuous process. As you grow in your sobriety journey, your needs might change, and your environment should evolve to reflect and support those changes. Regularly assess your space and make adjustments as necessary to ensure it remains a supportive foundation for your sobriety.

Transforming your environment isn't just about decoration or aesthetics; it's about creating a setting that continually nurtures your decision to live sober. It's a powerful step in reinforcing your day-to-day commitment to sobriety, providing a solid and supportive backdrop against which you can build a new, healthier life.

Take action today. Begin by looking around your space and

identifying one item you can change right now that will make your environment more supportive of your sobriety. Small steps lead to big changes, and every positive change in your environment is a stone in the foundation of your sober life.

By intentionally shaping your physical surroundings, you're not just arranging a space you're setting the stage for a successful, sustained recovery. Let each item in your space tell a story of health, happiness, and healing. Make your environment a mirror of the life you are building: clean, clear, and bright.

This journey might seem challenging at times, but remember, every element you adjust in your environment is a reflection of your inner strength and commitment to your sobriety. You are capable of creating a space that not only comforts but also empowers and inspires. So, keep going, one step at a time.

Chapter 8 Recap

Building a strong personal support system is key to reinforcing your journey towards sobriety. It's essential for maintaining the progress you've made and for providing a buffer against the challenges that might lead you astray. Let's take a look at the steps you can take to make sure your support system is as effective as it can be.

First, identifying supportive relationships is crucial. These are the relationships that will fuel your growth and help you stay on the path to sobriety. You need to evaluate the relationships you currently have. Ask yourself, which of these people support my sobriety? Which ones make me feel positive and encouraged? Once you identify these individuals, you make an effort to spend more time with them and less with those who might be harmful to your progress.

Next, fostering honest and open communication is vital. This means being real and open about your goals, struggles, and successes. When you share your journey openly, it not only helps you to stay accountable, it also strengthens the bonds within your support system. Encourage the same level of openness from others in your group, which can create a safe space for everyone to share and grow together.

Removing negative influences is another important step. This might mean having tough conversations or even distancing yourself from certain people. It's not easy, but it's necessary. Look at your social circles critically and be honest about who might be pulling you away from your goals. It might be tough at first, but setting clear boundaries is a form of self-respect and commitment to your sobriety.

Pay attention to environmental influences as well. The attitudes, beliefs, and behaviors of those around you can significantly impact your own mindset and actions. Try to surround yourself with positive influences and people who inspire you to be your best self. This could be through community groups, sober living environments, or even online forums and support networks.

Shaping your physical environment is also key. Create a living space that supports your sobriety. This might mean removing substances from your home, or it could involve designing a space that brings you peace and positivity. Whether it's hanging inspiring art, keeping your surroundings clean and organized, or setting up a special place for meditation or reflection, make your environment a sanctuary that supports your sobriety goals.

Here are some actionable steps you can take:

- Evaluate your friendships and relationships. Decide who truly supports your sober lifestyle.
- Communicate openly with your support network about your needs and progress.
- Distance yourself from people and situations that threaten your sobriety.
- Surround yourself with positive influences and create an environment that uplifts you.
- Modify your living space to eliminate triggers and enhance your mental peace.

Each of these steps plays a crucial role in building a support system that not only backs your commitment to stay sober but also enhances your overall quality of life. By following these guidelines, you're not just avoiding relapse; you're actively creating a lifestyle that supports your long-term well-being and sobriety.

Remember, the journey to sobriety isn't just about avoiding alcohol or other substances; it's about building a life where you don't feel the need to escape. Your support system is your foundation in this endeavor. With the right people around you and a suitable environment, you're better equipped to face the challenges and celebrate the successes on your path to a fulfilled and sober life.

CHAPTER NINE: PLAN AHEAD FOR SOBRIETY SUCCESS

Develop Strategies for Social Situations

When you decide to lead a sober life, social events can present a challenge. These gatherings often include alcohol, and navigating them without drinking requires a clear strategy. It's essential to prepare for these situations beforehand to maintain your commitment to sobriety.

First, think about the social events you will attend. These could be family gatherings, work events, or parties with friends. Understanding the setting and who will be there helps in planning your approach. It's good to know what to expect.

One effective strategy is to prepare responses for when someone offers you a drink. You might say, "I'm driving tonight," or "I'm taking a break from drinking." These responses are simple and usually do not invite further questions. It's helpful to practice these responses at home. Say them out loud in the mirror. This practice builds your confidence.

Another part of your strategy should include having a supportive companion with you at these events. Choose a friend or family member who understands your journey to sobriety. This person can help steer conversations away from drinking and provide moral support. You might even arrange a signal with them, like a nod or a text, if you need immediate support during the event.

Setting personal boundaries is also crucial. Decide in advance how long you will stay at the event. You can plan to arrive after any toasts or during a meal when drinking is not the main focus. Knowing your exit strategy beforehand can ease anxiety.

Self-care plays a big role in these strategies. Before going to an event, do something relaxing. Take a walk, listen to your favorite music, or meditate. Feeling calm and centered can help you handle the social pressure better. Wear something comfortable and something that makes you feel confident.

Finally, remember why you chose sobriety. Keeping your reasons in mind strengthens your resolve in challenging situations. Perhaps carry a small personal item that reminds you of your journey. It could be a bracelet, a ring, or a small note in your pocket.

These strategies are not just plans; they are tools that empower you to enjoy social events while staying true to your sober lifestyle. Each event you navigate successfully builds your confidence and reinforces your commitment to sobriety. Over time, these situations will become easier to manage as your new sober habits strengthen.

By preparing responses, having supportive companions, setting boundaries, practicing self-care, and remembering your reasons for sobriety, you equip yourself to face social situations without alcohol. This preparation is essential for anyone committed to a sober lifestyle, making each social event a victory in your journey to sobriety.

With each successful experience, you grow stronger in your resolve and more skilled in handling challenges. This growth is crucial to your sobriety journey, bringing you closer to a life where you can thrive without alcohol. Remember, every step you take is a step towards a healthier, happier you.

So, as you prepare for your next social event, review these strategies, practice them, and know that you are not just planning for a night out you are building a foundation for a lifetime of success in sobriety.

Each strategy you implement is a testament to your strength and commitment to your new life. This journey is not just about avoiding alcohol; it's about creating a life filled with meaningful interactions and true happiness. Keep pushing forward, and trust in your ability to navigate any situation soberly and successfully.

Remember, planning ahead isn't just about avoiding pitfalls; it's about creating a roadmap for success in every area of your life. With these strategies, you are ready to face social situations with confidence, grace, and resolve.

Stay strong, stay prepared, and continue to thrive in your sobriety. You have the tools, you have the strength, and you have the community to support you. Together, let's celebrate each step forward in this important journey.

Embrace these strategies, and watch as they transform not just your social experiences, but your entire approach to living soberly and joyfully.

Keep moving forward. You are capable of more than you know, and your sobriety journey is a powerful testament to your resilience and determination. Let these strategies guide you to success, one social event at a time.

By equipping yourself with these strategies, you are not only planning to succeed; you are ensuring a future where your sobriety is celebrated, respected, and fully integrated into every part of your life.

Together, let's continue to build a life of purpose, joy, and sobriety. With the right strategies, support, and mindset, every social situation becomes an opportunity to affirm your commitment to a healthier, happier you.

As you implement these strategies, remember that each small victory is a step towards a greater triumph in your sobriety journey. Celebrate each moment of success, learn from every challenge, and keep striving for the life you deserve one filled with joy, purpose, and sobriety.

Your journey is unique, and your strategies should reflect your personal goals and challenges. Tailor these approaches to fit your needs, and watch as you navigate social situations with increasing ease and confidence. Your sobriety is not just a path you've chosen; it's a celebration of your strength and commitment to a better life.

So, go ahead, plan with care, and step into each social event with the tools and confidence you need to maintain your sobriety. You've got this, and we are all here, cheering you on every step of the way. Let's make each social interaction a testament to your strength and a stepping stone towards lifelong sobriety success.

Find Fulfilling Alcohol-Free Activities

When thinking about sobriety, one of the key aspects is finding activities that are fulfilling and do not involve alcohol. This might seem challenging at first, especially if previous social gatherings or hobbies involved drinking. However, exploring new interests can be both refreshing and rewarding.

The first step is to consider what you enjoy doing or what you have always wanted to try. This can range from physical activities like joining a sports team, to more cerebral pursuits such as taking a class in photography or painting. The idea is to engage in activities that not only keep you occupied but also bring you joy and satisfaction.

Joining a sports team, for instance, is not just about the sport itself. It's about the camaraderie, the shared goals, and the routine of practice and games. Sports naturally boost your endorphins and serotonin levels, which are crucial for your mood and wellbeing. This makes sports a powerful, natural, and fun way to maintain sobriety.

Similarly, taking a class can be incredibly enriching. Learning something new stimulates your brain, provides a sense of achievement, and can open up new social networks. Whether it's cooking, writing, or learning a musical instrument, each class represents a step towards personal growth and away from old habits associated with alcohol.

Volunteering is another avenue to explore. It offers a sense of purpose and community connection, which are vital during sobriety. Helping at a local shelter, joining community clean-ups, or participating in charity events can make you feel needed and part of something bigger than yourself, reinforcing your commitment to sobriety.

It's important to prioritize these activities and make them a regular part of your life. They help establish a new routine, replacing the old one that included alcohol. Routine is comforting and can provide the structure needed during times of stress or when facing triggers.

Moreover, these activities connect you with people who may share similar interests and values, potentially leading to new friendships. These connections are invaluable as they create a support network around your new, sober lifestyle. Engaging with people who are supportive of your sobriety can make a significant difference in maintaining it.

To start, make a list of activities that interest you. It doesn't matter how small or big they are. The key is your interest and enjoyment. Experiment with different activities to see which ones fit best. It might take a few tries to find the right fit, but this is a normal part of the process.

Remember, the goal is to find joy and fulfillment without alcohol. This isn't just about distraction it's about rebuilding your life and making substantive changes that pave the way for long-term sobriety. Each new activity is a brick in the foundation of your new sober life, contributing not just to your hobbies but to your overall happiness and well-being.

In summary, finding fulfilling alcohol-free activities is a crucial step in maintaining sobriety. By focusing on what brings joy, personal growth, and connection, you can build a satisfying life that supports your sobriety goals. So take the time to explore and engage in new activities. Each step you take is a step towards a more fulfilled and sober life.

Understand and Replace Drinking Habits

Let's dive deep into the process of understanding and replacing your drinking habits. This is a crucial step for anyone looking to maintain sobriety and create a healthier lifestyle. First, understanding your drinking habits means recognizing what triggers your desire to drink. This could be a specific time of day, a particular emotional state, or even certain social situations. Everyone has different triggers, and pinpointing yours is fundamental.

Once you know what triggers your drinking, the next step is understanding the routine that follows. This might involve going to a specific place or engaging with particular people. It's often a predictable pattern that can be hard to break without a conscious effort. Understanding this routine is essential because it unveils the automatic process that leads to drinking, often without much conscious thought.

Now, think about the reward you get from drinking. It might be a feeling of relaxation, escape from stress, or simply the pleasure of taste and social interaction. Recognizing this reward is key because it's the reason the habit exists. The challenge here is finding alternative ways to achieve similar rewards without involving alcohol. This step is not about removing the reward but substituting the means of achieving it.

Let's talk about developing alternative routines. If your trigger is stress at work and your routine is having a drink right after work, change that routine. Instead of going to the bar, you could go to a gym or a park. This replaces the harmful routine with a healthy one while still addressing the reward relaxation and a break from stress.

These new routines should not feel like a punishment; they should be enjoyable and fulfilling. This could involve activities like sports, hobbies, or any interest that can engage you both physically and mentally. The key here is consistency. It takes time for new habits to become as ingrained as the old ones, so persistence is crucial.

It's also important to have coping mechanisms in place for those times when the urge to drink feels overwhelming. Strategies such as deep breathing, talking to a friend, or engaging in a distracting activity can be very effective. Over time, these new methods can help weaken the old triggers, making them less powerful, and your new routines more of a natural response.

To ensure these new habits stick, keep track of your triggers, routines, and rewards in a journal. Writing things down can make them clearer and easier to understand. It also helps you see progress over time, which is incredibly motivating. Celebrate small victories along the way each day without alcohol is an achievement.

In summary, replacing old drinking habits involves understanding the triggers, routines, and rewards that lead to alcohol consumption and deliberately replacing them with healthier alternatives that offer similar rewards. This process is not just about avoiding alcohol but about creating a lifestyle where the desire for alcohol naturally diminishes. It's about making choices that align with a healthier, happier you.

Remember, the goal here is to create a sustainable change that enhances your well-being without relying on alcohol. This journey is personal and can be challenging, but with commitment and the right strategies, it is entirely achievable. Embrace the process, be patient with yourself, and keep focused on your long-term goal of sobriety and improved quality of life.

Choose Enjoyable and Rewarding Alternatives

When you decide to live a life free from alcohol, it's essential to find new ways to spend your time that not only keep you engaged but also make you happy. This isn't just about keeping busy, but about discovering and doing things that truly bring joy and a sense of achievement to your life. Let's talk about how you can do exactly that.

Firstly, think about activities that you have always wanted to try but never did. Maybe you were interested in painting, learning to play a musical instrument, or trying your hand at gardening. These activities are not just ways to pass time; they are opportunities to grow new skills and passions. The joy and satisfaction that come from learning something new can be a powerful force in maintaining sobriety.

It's important to choose activities that you find genuinely enjoyable. If you don't enjoy the gym, don't force yourself to go just because it's a 'healthy' option. You might instead enjoy dancing, hiking, or swimming. The key is to engage in activities that feel like a treat, not a chore. This makes it more likely that you'll stick with them in the long run.

Next, think about incorporating social aspects into your new hobbies. Maybe you join a book club, a cooking class, or a local sports team. Connecting with others can not only make activities more enjoyable but can also provide a support network that is crucial in a sobriety journey. Sharing your experiences and challenges with others who are like-minded or in similar situations can provide comfort and encouragement.

Experimentation is also vital. You might not find the perfect activity right away, and that's okay. Try different things. Attend a pottery workshop one weekend, go to a community yoga class the next. Each experience will give you a better understanding of what you find enjoyable and fulfilling.

As you explore new hobbies, it's also important to create new routines that reinforce your sobriety. If Friday nights were previously a time for drinking, replace that habit with something equally rewarding. Perhaps every Friday evening could now be movie night, either with a group of friends at the cinema or a cozy setup at home. Or maybe it could be the time you volunteer at a local charity, helping others and enriching your own life in the process.

Remember, the alternatives you choose should not only be fun but should also give you a sense of accomplishment. This could be as simple as finishing a book every month, mastering a new recipe, or achieving a new fitness goal. Accomplishments, big or small, contribute to self-esteem and reinforce your commitment to sobriety.

Finally, be patient with yourself. Finding enjoyable and rewarding alternatives is a journey, not just a simple decision. It takes time to adjust to new activities and find what truly resonates with you. Keep trying new things, keep meeting new people, and keep exploring all the beautiful opportunities life has to offer. Your sobriety journey is unique to you, and so should be the activities that fill your time.

In conclusion, choosing activities and routines that are enjoyable and rewarding is crucial in your journey to sobriety. These activities not only help replace old habits but also provide new sources of joy and satisfaction. By experimenting and engaging in diverse and fulfilling activities, you enhance your ability to maintain a sober lifestyle that is vibrant, rewarding, and full of potential. Keep exploring, keep enjoying, and let each new activity strengthen the foundation of your sober life.

Align New Habits with Your Values

When you decide to live a life of sobriety, aligning your new habits with your personal values becomes crucial. Values act like a compass, guiding your decisions and behaviors. They reflect what is most important to you, shaping your actions and your life's direction. Choosing habits that resonate with your values not only makes maintaining these habits easier but also ensures they enhance your overall quality of life.

The process of alignment starts with understanding your own core values. Values such as honesty, integrity, health, family, or growth might be significant to you. Reflect on what truly matters in your life. This reflection can be as simple as listing things that make you feel purposeful and content. Think about times when you felt truly happy and fulfilled what were you doing? Who were you with? Answers to these questions can reveal a lot about your values.

Once you have a clear idea of your values, examine your new sober habits. Are these habits supporting your values? For instance, if 'health' is a core value, does your new exercise routine support this? If 'family' is important, do your activities enhance relationships with your loved ones? It's essential for your new habits to echo your values because this congruence brings harmony and reduces internal conflicts, making the sobriety journey smoother and more fulfilling.

Regular reassessment is also key. As you grow and change, your values might shift. What was important to you at the beginning of your sobriety journey might evolve. This change is natural and expected. Periodically checking to ensure that your habits still align with your values is crucial. It can be as simple as asking yourself every few months if your current routines and activities reflect what is most important to you and adjusting them as needed.

This alignment not only supports your sobriety but also enhances your overall well-being. When your daily actions and broader goals are in line with your personal values, there is a sense of peace and satisfaction that permeates your life. This satisfaction is incredibly beneficial in maintaining long-term sobriety, as it reduces the feelings of deprivation or missing out that can sometimes accompany the journey.

In practical terms, start small. Choose one value and one habit you want to align. If you value learning, perhaps start a new book or take a course on a subject that fascinates you. Make this activity a regular part of your routine. Over time, slowly add more aligned habits into your life, building a lifestyle that fully reflects your values. This gradual approach helps to ensure the changes are manageable and sustainable.

In conclusion, aligning your habits with your values is not just about making your sobriety journey easier it's about crafting a life you love and are proud of. It's about living authentically and fully. Each aligned habit is a step towards a more meaningful and satisfying life, a life where sobriety is not just about avoiding alcohol but about thriving in every sense of the word.

Chapter 9 Recap

When we talk about planning for a successful journey in sobriety, we emphasize the importance of being prepared. It's not just about knowing what to do; it's about having a clear strategy in place for different situations that might arise. This chapter has presented various strategies and actions that can help someone maintain their sobriety. Let's take a moment to summarize and reinforce these key points.

Firstly, let's talk about social situations, which can often be challenging for individuals striving to maintain sobriety. The approach here is proactive; it involves planning ahead. This means thinking about the kind of events you will attend, who will be there, and what kind of pressures you might face. Having a plan makes it much easier to say no to a drink. For instance, you could have a friend who knows your goals and can offer support throughout the event. Or, you could prepare a polite but firm way to decline a drink. It's about setting yourself up for success.

Finding fulfilling activities that do not involve alcohol is another crucial step. The idea is to replace the old habit of drinking with more positive and enriching activities. This could be sports, learning something new, or volunteering. These activities not only fill your time but also give you a sense of achievement and happiness that alcohol used to provide in an unhealthy way. It's about creating a new lifestyle that supports your sobriety.

Understanding and replacing your drinking habits involves a bit of introspection. Recognizing the triggers that make you want to drink is crucial. Once these are identified, you can begin to develop new routines that bypass or address these triggers. For example, if stress at work makes you feel like drinking, you could start practicing stress-relief techniques like meditation or regular exercise instead of turning to alcohol.

Choosing enjoyable and rewarding alternatives is about experimentation and discovery. It's important to try different activities to find what truly brings you joy and fulfillment. The goal is to find alternatives that are not just fillers but are genuinely rewarding. This makes the sober lifestyle not only manageable but enjoyable.

Finally, aligning your new habits with your values is about

ensuring your actions reflect what is truly important to you. This alignment supports sustained sobriety because your life reflects your deepest values, not temporary desires. It also involves continually reassessing your habits to ensure they still align with your goals as you grow and change over time.

The steps outlined here are actionable and specific. They serve as a roadmap that you can rely on in various scenarios:

- Prepare what to say before you find yourself in a situation where alcohol is offered.
- Identify activities that you enjoy and can do instead of attending events centered around alcohol.
- Recognize what triggers your desire to drink and have a plan for those moments.
- Test different sober activities and keep the ones that bring you the most fulfillment.
- Regularly review your lifestyle choices to ensure they align with your long-term goals.

By implementing these strategies, you're not just avoiding alcohol; you're building a life where alcohol no longer has a place. It's about creating a rich, fulfilling life that supports your sobriety. And remember, each step you take on this path strengthens your resolve and reinforces your ability to live soberly. The journey is continuous, and every action you take builds a stronger foundation for your sober life.

CHAPTER TEN: EMBRACE RESILIENCE AND ADAPTABILITY

Understand Setbacks as Part of the Process

When you're on a journey toward sobriety, it's vital to understand that setbacks are a normal part of this process. It's easy to feel discouraged when things don't go as planned. However, it's important to recognize that these moments do not define failure. Instead, they are part of the learning curve that everyone goes through.

Setbacks can come in various forms, such as a slip or a relapse, or maybe a particularly tough day where your old habits are calling you. It's crucial to see these not as roadblocks but as steps, albeit challenging ones, towards your goal.

Why is this perspective important? Because viewing setbacks as learning opportunities enables you to analyze what led to them. This analysis is critical. It helps you understand the triggers or circumstances that might lead to undesirable choices. By learning from each setback, you prepare yourself better for future challenges, thereby strengthening your ability to stay sober.

Think of it this way: every challenge you encounter and learn from adds a layer of strength to your commitment. Your journey to sobriety is not just about avoiding alcohol or other substances; it's about building a life where you can manage your desires and impulses effectively. This requires understanding, patience, and most importantly, resilience.

Resilience in this context means your ability to bounce back after a tough situation. The more you encounter these situations and come back from them, the more resilient you become. It's like exercising a muscle. The more you use it, the stronger it gets. Every time you overcome a setback, you're essentially telling yourself, "I can handle this, and I can do better next time."

Moreover, embracing setbacks as learning opportunities encourages a mindset shift. You start seeing these experiences not as failures but as integral, valuable parts of your journey. This mindset is empowering. It transforms your path to sobriety from a series of obstacles to a continual process of learning, growth, and personal development.

In practical terms, here is what you can do when faced with a setback:

1. Take a moment to acknowledge the situation. Understand what happened and accept that it is part of the journey.
2. Analyze the event. What triggered it? Was it a particular stressor? An event? A feeling? Identifying this can prevent future occurrences.
3. Reach out for support. Talk to a friend, a support group, or a counselor. Sharing your struggles can lighten your burden and provide you with different perspectives on handling the situation.
4. Reflect and learn. What can this setback teach you? Every challenge has a lesson. Find it, and use it to strengthen your resolve.
5. Adjust your plan. Maybe there's a need to tweak your strategies or add new ones. Adapt your approach based on what you've learned.

Seeing setbacks as opportunities for growth doesn't mean

they're easy to deal with. It's perfectly okay to feel upset or discouraged when they happen. However, it's crucial to remind yourself that each step back can lead to two steps forward if you learn from it and adjust accordingly.

Your sobriety journey is uniquely yours, and it's built on both your successes and your setbacks. By understanding and accepting setbacks as part of this process, you cultivate a sense of resilience that not only supports your journey to sobriety but also enriches your entire life experience. Remember, every day is a new opportunity to strengthen your commitment and move one step closer to a fulfilling, sober life.

To sum up, setbacks are not the end of the road; they are part of the journey. Learning from them builds resilience, empowers you, and enhances your ability to maintain your sobriety. Next time you face a challenge, remember, it's an opportunity to learn and grow stronger.

So, take each day as it comes. Be kind to yourself and remember that every experience has something valuable to offer. With this understanding, you are better equipped to handle whatever comes your way on this path to recovery.

Cultivate a Growth Mindset

Growth mindset is a powerful idea. It is the belief that you can improve your abilities and resilience through effort and learning. This belief is crucial, especially when you are on a journey like sobriety, where every step forward counts. Why is adopting a growth mindset so important? It changes how you view challenges and setbacks. Instead of seeing them as roadblocks, you can see them as opportunities to grow stronger and smarter.

Imagine you are learning to ride a bike. The first few tries might include falls and scraped knees. If you have a growth mindset, you don't see these falls as failures. Instead, you understand that with each fall, you learn something new about balancing and pedaling. Apply this to sobriety. Every challenge or setback is a chance to learn. Perhaps you learn about triggers or how to manage stress better. Every obstacle is a step forward because you gain knowledge and strength.

How do you cultivate a growth mindset? Start by recognizing that your brain can grow stronger and more capable with effort. When you face difficulties, remind yourself that each effort brings progress. This isn't just about feeling better; it's about building the mental muscles you need to support your sobriety.

Another step is to reframe obstacles. When something stands in your way, instead of thinking, "I can't do this," think, "What can I learn from this?" This small shift in thinking can turn a frustrating obstacle into a valuable lesson. Say you're invited to a social event where alcohol is present. Instead of fearing relapse, you could plan ways to support your sobriety, like bringing a sober friend or preparing responses to offers of drinks. Each obstacle then becomes a chance to practice and strengthen your sobriety skills.

Why is this mindset shift so crucial? It directly impacts your resilience the ability to bounce back from difficulties. With a growth mindset, you don't see setbacks as permanent or defining. Instead, they are temporary and educational. This perspective keeps you moving forward, even when the journey gets tough. You learn to push through barriers, not because it's easy, but because you know it's possible to come out stronger on the other side.

It's also helpful to celebrate small victories on your path to a growth mindset. Did you handle a stressful day without relying on old habits? That's a win. Celebrate it. These celebrations reinforce the belief that you are capable of growing and changing, which fuels your journey even further.

The practical application of a growth mindset in sobriety involves concrete steps. Each time you face a setback, take a moment to reflect. What did you learn? How can you use that knowledge next time? Write these reflections down. They are your evidence of growth. Over time, you'll see a clear record of how much you've learned and grown, which can be incredibly encouraging.

In summary, cultivating a growth mindset is about seeing every experience good or bad as a chance to grow. It's about believing in your ability to improve and using each challenge as a stepping stone. This approach not only supports your sobriety but also enriches your life, making you more resilient and adaptable no matter what comes your way. By embracing this mindset, you transform obstacles into opportunities to learn and strengthen yourself, ensuring that each step you take is grounded in growth and progress.

Practice Self-Compassion

When you are on a journey to maintain sobriety, treating yourself with kindness becomes essential. Think of it like being your own best friend. Let's talk about what this means and why it is so important.

Self-compassion means being gentle with yourself, especially when things don't go as planned. Suppose you encounter a setback. The kind and forgiving approach is not to criticize yourself harshly. Instead, talk to yourself like you would to a dear friend. You would not be harsh or critical to a friend, right? Extend that same courtesy to yourself.

Why is this important? When you're hard on yourself, it can lead to feelings of defeat and despair. These feelings might make it harder to stick to your sobriety goals. However, when you practice self-compassion, you create a supportive and encouraging space for yourself. This space helps you maintain your resolve and keep moving forward, even when mistakes happen.

Engaging in self-care activities is a practical way to practice self-compassion. What does self-care include? It involves any action that is done deliberately to take care of your mental, emotional, and physical health. This could be as simple as ensuring you get enough sleep, eating nutritious foods, or setting aside time for relaxation. These actions help strengthen you against stress and reduce the chance of relapse.

Positive self-talk is another crucial aspect of self-compassion. What we say to ourselves in our thoughts can significantly impact how we feel and behave. If you constantly think, "I can't do this," those thoughts can make it harder for you to progress. On the other hand, if your inner dialogue is more positive and supportive, saying things like, "I'm doing my best, and that's enough," it can boost your confidence and resilience.

How can you start practicing positive self-talk? Begin by noticing when negative thoughts creep in. When you catch yourself being critical, pause and try to reframe those thoughts in a more positive and kind way. Instead of thinking, "I messed up," you might say, "I made a mistake, but I can learn from it and try again." This shift in perspective can make a big difference in how you approach your sobriety journey.

In summary, practicing self-compassion involves treating yourself with kindness, engaging in self-care, and maintaining a positive inner dialogue. These actions are not just feel-good strategies; they are practical steps that can help you stay committed to your sobriety. Remember, being kind to yourself does not mean you are being indulgent or weak. It means you are giving yourself the same respect and care you would offer to someone you love, and it is a crucial part of your path to long-term sobriety.

By adopting a compassionate approach towards yourself, you enhance your ability to face and overcome the challenges that come with maintaining sobriety. This self-kindness leads to a healthier mental state, reduces stress, and fosters resilience, making your recovery journey smoother and more sustainable.

Develop a Contingency Plan

When you're on a journey to maintain sobriety, it's important to prepare for moments that might test your resolve. Think of it like having a safety net. A contingency plan serves as your safety net. It's a plan that you create in advance, detailing what you will do in high-risk situations. These are situations or moments when you're likely to face triggers or potential setbacks in your commitment to sobriety.

First, let's consider what high-risk situations might look like. These could be events or places where alcohol is present, times of significant emotional distress, or even periods of major celebration. Recognizing these situations beforehand is the first step in your planning.

Next, you need to outline specific coping strategies. These are your tools to handle challenging moments without compromising your sobriety. Coping strategies can be various. For example, some people find that calling a supportive friend or family member helps. Others might find it beneficial to remove themselves from the triggering environment immediately.

Along with personal coping strategies, it's essential to have a list of support resources. These resources might include contact information for your therapist, a sobriety support group, or a helpline number. It's like having a list of people and places you can turn to when you need help. This part of your plan ensures that you're not dealing with these situations alone.

Emergency contacts are a critical part of your contingency plan. These are the people who know about your journey and are ready to provide support when you reach out. Having these contacts saved on your phone, or even written down somewhere easily accessible, ensures that in moments of weakness, you don't have to think too hard about whom to call. You have already made this decision when you were in a calm and rational state of mind.

It's also useful to write down your reasons for staying sober and read them during challenging times. This might seem simple, but reminding yourself why you started this path can be a powerful motivator to stay on track when faced with temptation or stress.

Lastly, practice going through your contingency plan. Just like a fire drill, practicing your responses to various scenarios can make you feel more confident and prepared. It helps to reduce panic and hasty decisions because you've already run through what needs to be done. You know the steps, and you just need to follow them.

In summary, developing a contingency plan involves recognizing high-risk situations, outlining specific coping strategies, listing support resources, and identifying emergency contacts. It also involves reminding yourself about your reasons for choosing sobriety and practicing your plan to ensure familiarity and ease of execution. By having this plan in place, you empower yourself to maintain your commitment to sobriety, even when faced with difficulties. This is a practical and actionable way to support your journey, making sure that the path you've chosen remains clear and achievable.

Remember, the goal of the contingency plan is not just to avoid relapse but to manage challenges in such a way that they strengthen your commitment and enhance your ability to navigate the journey of sobriety with confidence and support.

Celebrate Your Progress and Resilience

Throughout your journey to maintain sobriety, there are many moments that could be easy to overlook. However, celebrating your progress and the resilience you demonstrate during these times is crucial. It's important to focus on how far you've come rather than how far you have to go.

Let's begin by understanding what it means to celebrate your progress. Every step you take on this journey, whether big or small, is a victory. These steps could be as simple as resisting a craving or reaching a sobriety milestone. Acknowledging these achievements is not just about giving yourself a pat on the back. It's about reinforcing your belief in your ability to change and acknowledging your growth. This recognition is what fuels your journey forward.

Now, why focus on resilience? Resilience in the context of sobriety means your ability to bounce back from challenges and setbacks without reverting to old habits. It's about learning from each experience and using that knowledge to strengthen your resolve. Sobriety is not a linear path; it has its ups and downs. By celebrating your resilience, you remind yourself that you are capable of overcoming difficulties and maintaining your path to recovery.

How do you celebrate these achievements? Start with setting clear milestones. These could be related to the duration of sobriety, like one week, one month, or one year without alcohol. They could also be related to personal growth, such as successfully handling a situation that would have previously triggered you to drink.

Once you have these milestones, think about ways to celebrate that feel meaningful to you. This could be a small family gathering, a quiet evening with a book, or a special purchase you've been saving for. The key is to choose celebrations that reinforce your new lifestyle rather than contradict it. For instance, instead of going to a bar, you could go to a favorite restaurant or plan a trip to a place you've always wanted to visit.

It's also helpful to share your successes with supportive friends, family, or members of your support group. Sharing not only allows you to celebrate together but also strengthens your support network. It reinforces the idea that your journey matters to others too. Plus, it can inspire and motivate others on their paths.

In addition to planned celebrations, it's important to cultivate daily gratitude. Each day, take a moment to reflect on something positive about your journey. Maybe you handled a stressful moment at work without feeling the urge to drink, or perhaps you were able to offer support to someone else in their sobriety journey. Recognizing these daily wins keeps your mindset positive and focused on recovery.

Remember, the path to sobriety is as much about the journey as it is about the destination. By celebrating your progress and resilience, you're not just marking milestones; you're building a foundation of positive experiences and memories that reinforce your sobriety. Each celebration is a building block in a new lifestyle, one in which you're continuously learning, growing, and succeeding.

So, take the time to acknowledge and celebrate your achievements. This practice will not only enhance your sense of fulfillment but will also significantly contribute to your long-term commitment to sobriety. Celebrating your progress and resilience shows that you value yourself and your journey. It sends a powerful message to yourself and the world about the importance of your health and happiness. This, in essence, is a key component to a sustainable recovery and a joyful, fulfilling life.

As you continue on your journey, keep these ideas in mind. Every step forward, no matter how small, is a step towards a healthier, more resilient you. Celebrate each moment of strength, each day of progress, and each milestone reached. These celebrations not only brighten your days but also solidify your path on the journey of sobriety, reinforcing the message that every effort is worthwhile and that you are truly evolving.

Chapter 10 Recap

When we talk about embracing resilience and adaptability, we're discussing core strengths that are crucial in your sobriety journey. Each step in this chapter aims to bolster your ability to handle setbacks, grow from them, and celebrate the significant strides you make along the way. Let's explore why each of these concepts is important and how you can implement actionable steps to make them part of your life.

Firstly, understanding setbacks as part of the process is essential. It's common to face challenges when you are committed to maintaining sobriety. These aren't signs of failure but are, in fact, opportunities to learn and strengthen your commitment. When a setback occurs, it's helpful to step back and analyze what led to it. Was it a particular stressor? An unexpected event? Understanding these triggers helps you prepare better for future challenges.

How can you turn this understanding into action? Start by keeping a journal of your sobriety journey. Whenever you experience a setback, write down what happened and think about what might have triggered it. This makes it easier to identify patterns and prepare strategies for similar situations in the future. Also, discuss these setbacks with a therapist or a support group. This not only helps you gain perspectives but also reinforces your support network.

Next, cultivating a growth mindset is about believing that your abilities to manage sobriety can be strengthened through effort and learning. This mindset empowers you to view challenges as opportunities to enhance your skills and coping strategies. To cultivate a growth mindset, focus on learning from each experience. Instead of getting discouraged by difficulties, ask yourself, "What can I learn from this?" This approach shifts your focus from what went wrong to how you can improve.

To make this practical, set specific, small learning goals for your sobriety each week. Perhaps you want to learn more about stress management techniques or find new activities that reduce cravings. As you achieve each small goal, you'll build confidence in your ability to handle bigger challenges.

Practicing self-compassion involves treating yourself with

kindness and understanding during tough times. It's easy to be hard on yourself, but harsh self-criticism can derail your sobriety efforts. Instead, engage in positive self-talk. Remind yourself that recovery is a journey and that it's okay to have difficult days.

Actionably, you can practice self-compassion by starting each day with a positive affirmation related to your sobriety. Something as simple as saying, "I am doing my best, and that's enough," can set a supportive tone for the day. Additionally, when you face a tough day, treat yourself to a comforting activity, like reading a favorite book or taking a walk in nature.

Developing a contingency plan is about being prepared. Imagine you're going to a place or event where you know there will be alcohol. Having a plan in place can help you stay on track. Your plan should include what you will do in case you feel tempted and who you will call if you need support.

Create this plan by listing potential high-risk situations and your strategies for handling them. Share this plan with a trusted friend or your support group members so they can help keep you accountable and provide support when needed.

Finally, celebrating your progress and resilience is vital. It's important to acknowledge your successes, no matter how small. This not only boosts your morale but also strengthens your commitment to sobriety.

Make it a habit to celebrate your milestones. Set up a reward system for yourself; for instance, after a month of sobriety, treat yourself to a movie night or a new book. Share your successes with friends, family, or your support group as well. Celebrating with others can make the experience more meaningful and reaffirming.

In conclusion, embracing resilience and adaptability in your sobriety journey means understanding setbacks as part of the process, cultivating a growth mindset, practicing self-compassion, developing a contingency plan, and celebrating your progress. These steps are not just theories but are practical, actionable strategies that can strengthen your journey towards a sustained sobriety. Each step builds on the last, creating a robust framework that supports your growth and recovery. Remember, each day is a step forward, and every challenge is an opportunity to learn and become stronger.

CONCLUSION: RECAP OF CORE CONCEPTS

Embracing 100% Commitment to Sobriety

When you choose to live sober, the first step is to commit fully. This means you've firmly decided not to drink alcohol ever again for the rest of your life. You take charge of your journey. This full responsibility is not easy, but it's crucial for success. It's about saying, "I am in control" and believing it.

Every choice, every day, has to support this commitment. This might mean changing habits or avoiding places where you used to drink. It's all part of making sure you stay on your sober path.

Being 100% committed helps you stand firm against challenges. When you're fully committed, you're more likely to keep going, even when it's tough. This commitment is your foundation.

Announcing Your Sobriety Goal

Telling someone else about your goal to stay sober is a big step. This person can help keep you on track. Choose someone who supports and cares about your well-being. This could be a friend, family member, or a professional who understands addiction.

When you share your goal, it becomes real. It's no longer just a thought. Announcing your goal adds a layer of accountability. It's like saying, "I'm serious about this, and I need your help to make it happen."

This accountability is a powerful tool. It means someone else knows about your commitment and can offer support and encouragement. They can also help you stay honest about your progress.

Engaging in Daily Journaling

Journaling every day is a helpful way to understand your feelings and track your progress. It's a private space where you can express yourself freely. Writing down your thoughts and experiences helps you see how far you've come. It also helps you recognize patterns or triggers in your behavior.

This daily record is more than just a diary. It's a tool for reflection and growth. It can show you your strengths and the areas where you need more support. Journaling is a stress reliever too. It allows you to unload emotions safely on paper.

As you continue to write daily, you'll create a valuable resource you can look back on. This helps in understanding the journey better and planning future steps in maintaining sobriety.

Practicing Gratitude

Gratitude is about focusing on the good things in your life. It could be simple things like having a home or the support of loved ones. Recognizing these blessings can shift your mindset to a more positive outlook.

Practicing gratitude daily makes you appreciate life more. It reduces feelings of envy or regret by reminding you of what you have, not what you lack. This positive mindset supports sobriety by fostering happiness and satisfaction with your life as it is now, without alcohol.

Simple gratitude practices include keeping a gratitude journal or just taking a moment each day to think about things you're thankful for. These acts of thankfulness bring inner peace and joy, essential for recovery.

Gratitude affirmations are specialized forms of positive affirmation. Gratitude is an outward expression. When you're grateful, you acknowledge the goodness around you, like a great sunrise or cup of coffee, not waking up hungover. Gratitude affirmations are outward, and positive affirmations are inward. Both play vital roles in positive self-concept. They are your sword and shield against alcoholism and the daily stresses that bombard you from all directions. Use these affirmation techniques daily to create a bulletproof mindset. This works in all areas of life.

Gratitude affirmations and positive affirmations serve different yet equally important purposes. The former focuses outward, while the latter focuses inward. Together, they are essential for nurturing a positive self-concept, helping you navigate the challenges of alcoholism and the daily stresses of modern life.

Embracing Forgiveness

Forgiveness is letting go of anger and resentment. This is not just forgiving others, but also forgiving yourself. Holding onto past hurts or mistakes can hold you back from moving forward in sobriety.

Forgiving doesn't mean forgetting. It means accepting what happened and finding a way to live with it peacefully. This release can lead to healing and growth. It's about setting yourself free from negative emotions that can lead to relapse.

Embracing forgiveness improves your mental health and

strengthens your resolve to stay sober. It's an act of kindness to yourself and others, paving the way for rebuilt relationships and personal peace.

Harnessing the Power of Visualization

Visualization is a technique where you picture yourself succeeding in your mind. Imagine yourself living a fulfilled, sober life. These mental images can inspire and motivate you.

By visualizing your goals, you connect emotionally to the outcomes you desire. This emotional connection makes the goals feel more real and achievable. It's like practicing success in your mind before it happens.

Use visualization to prepare for challenging situations. Picture yourself handling these situations with calm and confidence. This mental rehearsal can make you feel more prepared when you face these challenges in real life.

Utilizing Positive Affirmations

Positive affirmations are short, powerful statements that you repeat to yourself. They help you overcome negative thoughts and reinforce your commitment to sobriety. These affirmations reprogram your mind to believe in your ability to stay sober.

Examples of affirmations might include "I am strong enough to overcome my addiction" or "Every day, in every way, I'm getting better and stronger." Repeating these daily strengthens your mental resolve and self-belief.

Positive affirmations are simple yet powerful tools that can shift your mindset, boost your confidence, and support your sobriety goals.

Building a Personal Support System

A support system includes people who support and encourage your sobriety. This could be family, friends, therapists, or personal support group. These people provide encouragement, advice, and understanding.

Building a network of supportive relationships is crucial. This network can offer practical help, like someone to call when you're feeling tempted, or emotional support during tough times. Positive influences help you stay focused and optimistic.

Choose people who respect your decision to remain sober and who positively influence your life. Avoid relationships that are toxic or lead to temptation.

Planning Ahead

Planning ahead involves thinking about potential challenges and deciding how to handle them before they happen. This could mean avoiding certain social situations or finding new ways to enjoy socializing without alcohol.

Strategies might include having a non-alcoholic drink in hand at parties or planning an exit strategy if you start to feel uncomfortable. Being prepared reduces anxiety and increases your confidence in maintaining sobriety.

By planning, you create a safety net that helps you navigate through situations that might otherwise jeopardize your sobriety.

Embracing Resilience and Adaptability

Finally, being resilient means bouncing back from setbacks without giving up on your sobriety goals. Adaptability is about adjusting your strategies as needed.

Setbacks are part of the journey. Learning from them and continuing to move forward is key. Being adaptable means being willing to try new strategies if the old ones aren't working as well anymore.

Resilience and adaptability are not just about recovering from setbacks. They're about learning, growing, and becoming stronger through the challenges. This strength supports your long-term sobriety.

All these concepts are tools in your toolbox for sobriety. They work together to build a strong foundation, keep you moving forward, and help you live a fulfilling sober life. Now, it's up to you to use these tools daily and make your journey a successful one.

Encouragement to Take Action

Now, it's essential to realize the transformative power that lies within the strategies we've discussed. When you consistently apply these methods toward your goal of sobriety, you invoke a strength within yourself that can profoundly change your life.

Consider this: each strategy is a step, and every step you take is a move towards a healthier, more fulfilling life. It isn't just about avoiding alcohol; it's about building a life where alcohol no longer has a place or a say.

Imagine waking up each morning feeling clear-headed and

motivated. Picture yourself building stronger, more authentic relationships with your friends and family. Think about the pride that comes with each sober day, knowing every moment is lived fully and truly. These aren't just possible outcomes; they can be your reality if you continue to take action on what you've learned.

Let's focus on the benefits of a sober lifestyle for a moment. Improved health is one of the most straightforward benefits. Without alcohol, your body can function better, your liver gets a break, and your brain can heal and work more efficiently. But the benefits extend beyond the physical. Your mental health can improve significantly, reducing anxiety and depression, which often coexist with alcohol abuse.

Then, there's your personal and professional life. Sobriety can enhance your ability to perform at work, be present for your loved ones, and engage in hobbies and activities you truly enjoy. These aren't minor changes. They're transformative and can shift the trajectory of your life toward more positive outcomes.

But these outcomes hinge on consistent action. It's not enough to understand the strategies; you must live them. Every day provides a new opportunity to reinforce your commitment, whether it's through journaling, engaging in visualization, or affirming your strength and resilience through positive self-talk.

Let's not overlook the emotional and psychological benefits. Gaining control over your life, feeling empowered by your decisions rather than controlled by a substance, changes more than just your daily habits it changes the way you see yourself and your future.

You might find yourself taking on challenges you never thought possible, pursuing goals that seemed out of reach while under the influence of alcohol. Each step in your sober journey is a step towards realizing your potential.

Remember, while the journey is deeply personal, you're not walking this path alone. Every action you take builds bridges to others through shared experiences, through the support system you build, and through the positive influence you become on others' lives.

Let each day be a building block towards that future. Make your actions today reflect the life you want for yourself tomorrow. If you're ever in doubt, remember why you started. Reflect on the benefits you've already begun to experience, and let that motivate you to press on, even when it's tough.

Your journey to sobriety is not just about leaving alcohol behind; it's about embracing a fuller, more vibrant life. It's about becoming the best version of yourself. With every strategy you apply, you're not just avoiding alcohol; you're creating a life where you thrive.

So, take a deep breath. Let's keep moving forward, step by step, day by day. Keep applying what you've learned, and let your actions today build a brighter, sober tomorrow.

Yes, the road might feel long and at times difficult, but the rewards of a sober life a life of clarity, achievement, and deeper connections are worth every step. Embrace the challenge with an open heart and an open mind. Continue to take deliberate, consistent actions towards your sobriety. It's within your reach to transform your life, and it starts with every small, determined step you take.

To conclude, your active participation in this transformative journey is essential. Sobriety isn't merely the absence of alcohol; it is the presence of a healthier, more engaged, and fulfilling life.

Every strategy, every effort, and every day counts. Keep pushing forward, keep staying true to your course, and let each day be a testament to your resilience and commitment to your sobriety.

Actionable Takeaways

Starting a journey towards a sober life demands clarity and definitive actions. To begin, creating a specific and measurable goal for your sobriety is essential. This goal isn't just a vague wish; it should be a concrete milestone you can aim for and measure your progress against. For instance, you might decide to stay sober for the next 30 days. Whatever your goal, it's critical to articulate it in clear terms.

Once your goal is set, sharing it with someone you trust an accountability partner is your next step. This should be a person who supports your journey and can provide motivation and encouragement when challenges arise. Choose someone who will check in on you, offer constructive feedback, and celebrate your successes along the way.

Journaling daily is another powerful tool. It helps you process emotions, reflect on your experiences, and track your progress toward your sobriety goal. Every day, spend some time writing about your feelings, the challenges you encountered, how you overcame them, and any thoughts about your sobriety journey. This practice offers you insights into patterns and triggers, helping you manage them more effectively.

Gratitude, visualization, and affirmations are exercises that should also be part of your daily routine. Set aside time each morning or evening for these activities. Practicing gratitude can be as simple as writing down three things you are thankful for each day. Visualization involves closing your eyes and picturing yourself successfully living a sober life, experiencing the benefits it brings. Affirmations are positive statements you repeat to yourself, designed to boost your confidence and reinforce your commitment to sobriety.

Assessing and adjusting your social circle and environment also play a pivotal role in supporting your sobriety. If certain places or groups of people increase your temptation to drink, it may be necessary to distance yourself from those triggers. Surround yourself with positive influences and environments that promote and support your new lifestyle. This might mean making new friends, finding sober communities, or changing your routines to avoid old habits.

Developing a personalized plan to handle triggers is also crucial. This plan should include strategies for dealing with social situations where alcohol is present and finding healthy, enjoyable alternatives to drinking. By preparing in advance, you can navigate these challenges more successfully and stay on track with your sobriety goals.

Finally, remember to acknowledge and celebrate your progress. Recognizing the milestones, you reach and the obstacles you overcome reinforces your commitment and resilience. Maintaining a growth mindset viewing setbacks as opportunities to learn and strengthen your resolve is essential for long-term success.

To encapsulate, the path to sobriety is not just about abstaining from alcohol; it's about setting clear goals, engaging in regular self-reflection and exercises, adjusting your social dynamics, planning for triggers, and celebrating your journey. Each of these steps plays a vital role in building a solid foundation for a sober life, aligned with the principles laid out throughout this book: embracing responsibility, cultivating positive habits, and establishing supportive networks. By implementing these actionable steps, you empower yourself to maintain sobriety and enjoy a fulfilling, alcohol-free life.

Call to Action

Now is the time to take a step forward in your journey to sobriety. Each choice you make today shapes your tomorrow. You've learned many strategies within these pages that can help you live a sober life. It's time to put these into action, right now. Start by selecting one strategy from the book that resonates with you. Maybe it's writing in a journal daily or perhaps it's practicing gratitude each morning. Choose one to start with. This is important because starting with too many changes at once can be overwhelming. By focusing on one strategy, you can dedicate your energy to creating a new habit that supports your sobriety.

Once you've chosen your strategy, commit to it. How do you commit? You write it down. Get a piece of paper and a pen. Write, "I commit to [insert strategy] every day to support my sobriety." Place this commitment where you can see it every day. This might be on your refrigerator, by your bed, or on the bathroom mirror. Seeing your commitment daily helps remind you of the decision you've made to change.

Next, tell someone about your commitment. This could be a friend, family member, or a supportive community member who understands your journey. Sharing your goal not only makes it more real but also holds you accountable. Let them know why this change is important to you and how it will help you in your sobriety. They can offer support and encouragement, which can make a big difference on tough days. If you're feeling unsure about making these changes on your own, or if you need more guidance, consider joining a support group. Support groups provide not only guidance but also the companionship of others who are on similar paths. This can be incredibly comforting and motivating. If you're not sure where to find a group, look back at the resources section of this book for suggestions. You can also search online for groups in your area or find virtual meetings that you can join from anywhere.

Additionally, you might find it helpful to reach out for professional help. This could be a counselor or therapist who specializes in addiction and sobriety. Working with a professional can provide you with personalized strategies and support tailored to your specific needs. Remember, taking action is what brings about change. While learning new strategies and understanding the principles of sobriety are crucial, the real transformation happens when you apply what you've learned. Every small step you take is a part of your larger journey to recovery.

Finally, celebrate every victory, no matter how small. Every day that you stick to your commitment is an achievement. Celebrate these moments. They are proof of your strength and determination. Sobriety is not just about avoiding alcohol; it's about creating a life filled with meaningful actions and relationships that support your overall well-being. Implementing these strategies requires courage and effort, but remember, you are not alone in this journey. Every step you take is a step towards a healthier, more fulfilling life. Take that step now. You have the tools and the knowledge. Make the choice to use them. Start today.

This call to action isn't just about following steps; it's about transforming your life. It's about moving from knowledge to action. From intention to practice. So, embrace this moment as the start of something new. Use the strategies that resonate with you, reach out when you need help, and build a network of support that will journey with you. Sobriety is within reach, and it starts with your decision to act today.

Resources

As we conclude this journey of understanding sobriety, it's important to equip you with tools that will continuously support and inspire your growth. In this section, we'll explore various resources that you can tap into to deepen your knowledge, gain more insights, and stay motivated on your path to sobriety.

Books are a great way to start. They can offer comprehensive insights and personal stories that resonate with your experiences. Here are some recommend

Annie Grace's This Naked Mind by Annie Grace: This Naked Mind offers a new solution. Packed with surprising insight into the reasons we drink, it will open your eyes to the startling role of alcohol in our culture.

Allen Carr's Quit Drinking Without Willpower: Allen Carr's Easy way method has been applied to problem drinking. By explaining why, you feel the need to drink and with simple step-by-step instructions to set you free, he shows you how to escape from the alcohol trap.

Listening to podcasts is another excellent way to fill your moments with motivational and educational content. Here are a few podcasts that might be helpful.

The Addicted Mind Podcast: Is about understanding addiction, its impact and the latest treatment options available.

This podcast aims to create an environment of compassion for individuals caught in the destructive grip of the addictive process. It works to deliver real hope to people who are suffering from addiction's painful impact.

The ODAAT Chat Podcast: Is about recovery from alcoholism, drug addiction, sobriety and the journey of recovery, community and healing. Guests tell their stories of what it was like, what happened and where they are now. The recovery stories they share are inspiring, funny and touching, providing hope to help others feel like they are not alone.

Staying informed and connected can also come from digital platforms and support groups. Consider these websites and online communities:

Support Groups

LifeRing: lifering.org

Rational Recovery

rational.org

Secular Organizations for Sobriety: cfiwest.org/sos

Smart Recovery: smartrecovery.org

Women for Sobriety: womenforsobriety.org

An online community where you can share your journey and learn from other's experiences in a supportive environment.

All these resources are designed to provide you with a variety of perspectives and tools. Whether you prefer reading, listening, or interactive engagement, there is something here that can meet your needs and suit your preferences. Remember, the goal is not just to stay sober but to thrive in sobriety. Utilizing these resources can help you build a robust framework for your life, keeping you inspired and informed as you journey through recovery.

As you explore these options, consider what resonates most with your personal learning style and recovery needs. Engage with these resources actively and reflect on their teachings. Apply what you learn in a way that complements the strategies and insights you've gained from this book. Continuously enriching your understanding and strategies for sobriety will empower you to maintain your course and achieve the fulfilling, sober life you are working towards.

www.ingramcontent.com/pod-product-compliance
Lightning Source LLC
Chambersburg PA
CBHW071356120626
46546CB00002B/711